Graham Handley MA PH D

Brodie's Notes on John Steinbeck's

Of Mice and Men
and The Pearl

Pan Books London and Sydney

First published 1977 by Pan Books Ltd
Cavaye Place, London SW10 9PG

   3   4   5   6   7   8   9

© Graham Handley 1977

ISBN 0 330 50066 X

Printed and bound in Great Britain by
Richard Clay (The Chaucer Press) Ltd, Bungay, Suffolk

Contents

Page references in these Notes are to the Pan edition of
Of Mice and Men and *The Pearl*, but references are usually
given to particular parts and chapters, so that the Notes
may be used with any edition of the book

Letters quoted are taken from *Steinbeck: A Life in Letters*
(published by Pan Books)

To the student

A close reading of the set books is the student's primary task. These Notes will help to increase your understanding and appreciation of the two short stories, and to stimulate *your own* thinking about them. *The Notes are in no way intended as a substitute* for a thorough knowledge of the books.

The author and his work

John Steinbeck was born on 27 February 1902, in Salinas, California, the third of four children. He was later to observe that his parents had plenty of land, which was liable to give people the idea that they were rich whereas in fact they were often poor; but 'lords of the land, you know, and really low church mice but proud'. By 1919 he had graduated from high school and had begun to attend Stanford University, but he took a number of jobs in the course of his college career. One of these jobs was as a ranch-hand near King City, and both the experience and the setting were later to be used with a particular sharpness of focus in *Of Mice and Men*; he also worked as a clerk, served in a haberdashery store and in a café, broke in army remounts for 'officers' gentle behinds', and also did night shifts loading and stacking sacks of sugar. But he was passionately interested in reading, and early determined to become a writer. In 1924 he published two stories in the Stanford *Spectator*, but there was no overnight success, and his voluminous letters convey the sense of his early struggles and the gradual upward trend of his literary and material fortunes.

He read French, Spanish and Russian classics as well as keeping abreast of significant current literature. He worked variously on the West Coast from 1926 to 1928 more particularly in the Lake Tahoe area, doing odd jobs. His first novel, *Cup of Gold*, was published in 1929, and was an account, suitably fictionalized, of the buccaneer Sir Henry Morgan. The book had been rejected altogether seven times before reaching print. In 1930 he married Carol Henning, and moved to a cottage at Pacific Grove, on the Monterey Peninsula, where he settled; he was to return to this home throughout his life. In 1931 he first came into contact with McIntosh and Otis, who were from then on to remain his literary agents for the rest of his writing career. His early stories, set in the Californian valleys he knew so well, were published in 1932 under the title of *The Pastures of Heaven* (his agents, he said, 'palmed off *The Pastures* on somebody'). Meanwhile, his wife began to work in the laboratory of Edward F. Ricketts, marine biologist and philosopher, and much more besides: Ricketts was to become Steinbeck's close friend and collaborator, whose thinking and way of life were to exert a great influence upon him.

To a God Unknown and the first two parts of *The Red Pony* were published in 1933; followed by a short story (in 1934), 'The Murder'; and then his first great success, *Tortilla Flat* (1935). His strike novel, *In Dubious Battle*, appeared in 1936. In the same year he began work on the short novel which was to rank as one of his masterpieces, *Of Mice and Men*: it was published in 1937 and successfully dramatized, winning a Drama Critics Award. In the same year *The Red Pony*, in three parts, was also issued: the fourth part of *The Red Pony* and *The Long Valley* appeared in 1938. And in 1939 came the most ambitious venture yet, *The Grapes of Wrath*. This novel, as Walter Allen has pointed out, 'includes within itself a considerable part, however dramatically or melodramatically heightened, of the experience of a considerable number of Americans during the thirties'. Meanwhile, *Tortilla Flat* was filmed.

Steinbeck was now something of a success, with all the attendant perils accruing to his status: many letters, autograph hunters, attacks from farmers and landowners, who accused him of being a Communist and a liar – as well as the adverse publicity of a woman claiming to be pregnant by him! Throughout, he was becomingly modest: he had worked very hard on *The Grapes of Wrath*, and had even advised printing a small edition since he was convinced that it would not be a success. Much of its language was toned down by his agent,

Elizabeth Otis, but Steinbeck refused to compromise on the ending, in which Rose of Sharon gives her breast to the starving man. In his own words, 'I tried to write this book the way lives are being lived not the way books are written'. He gave the manuscript to his wife.

In June 1939 the film rights of *Of Mice and Men* and *The Grapes of Wrath* had been sold, the films of the two books being released in 1939 and 1940 respectively, and in the latter year Steinbeck was awarded the Pulitzer prize for *The Grapes of Wrath*. In 1941 he set off on a marine biology expedition with Ed Ricketts; he had always been interested in human existence in its biological aspects, and the fruits of the trip are to be found in *The Log from the Sea of Cortez* and, though almost more of a by-product, *The Pearl*. Meanwhile his marriage to Carol was breaking up; they were divorced in 1942; and in 1943 he married Gwyndolyn Conger. In the meantime he had completed a novel set in unspecified but occupied territory, *The Moon is Down*, which was also successfully dramatized. In 1943 he went to Europe as war correspondent for the *New York Herald Tribune*; early in 1944 he saw the film, *Lifeboat*, which he had written and which was directed by Alfred Hitchcock, but Steinbeck objected to what he considered distortion in the final version of the script. In the same year another of his great successes, *Cannery Row*, was published. By the beginning of 1945 he had practically finished *The Pearl*, of which he said, 'It's a brutal story but with flashes of beauty I think'. This too was filmed, as was *The Wayward Bus*, which came out in 1947. In 1948 his close friend, Ed Ricketts, died following a car crash; and, as Steinbeck was later to write, so acutely did he feel the loss, 'It wasn't Ed who had died but a large and important part of oneself'. In the same year his second wife decided that she wanted a divorce; and, by one of Fate's ironies he was at the same time elected to the American Academy of Arts and Letters. In 1949, he met and fell in love with Elaine Scott, who was to become his third wife, and continued to work on film scripts. He married Elaine in 1950 and published a novel, *Burning Bright*, which was followed in 1951 by *The Log from the Sea of Cortez*.

East of Eden came out in 1952, while in 1954 Steinbeck lived abroad for some months, acting as correspondent for *Le Figaro*, Paris. *Sweet Thursday* was published in the same year, and it was made into a musical in 1955; 1957 saw *The Short Reign of Pippin IV* completed. Steinbeck had always been interested in the Arthurian legends – more particularly the work of Malory – and travelled to Italy to study material there. *Once There Was A War* was published in 1958, but he returned to his obsession with *Morte D'Arthur*, saying 'If Malory could re-write Chrétien for his time, I can re-write Malory for mine'. Thus he spent most of 1959 in Somerset working on *Morte D'Arthur*. It was a fascinating and, for him, compulsive experience, and he wrote to Robert Bolt, who had found him the cottage he was staying in, 'Words are truly people, magic people, having birth, growth and destiny'. In 1960 he travelled throughout America, collecting material for the book which was to be called *Travels With Charley*, and in 1961 his last novel, *The Winter of Our Discontent*, was published. In 1962 Steinbeck was awarded the Nobel Prize for Literature; in 1963 he travelled in Eastern Europe and Russia, and was in Warsaw when President Kennedy was assassinated. His letters to Mrs Kennedy (now Jacqueline Onassis) are moving and wise; and she in her turn wrote, much later, to Elaine Steinbeck, 'His letters say more than a whole book could – I will treasure them all my life.' In 1964 Steinbeck was awarded the Presidential Medal of Freedom, and he closely supported the policies of Kennedy's successor, Lyndon B. Johnson. He saw his second son depart for war service in Vietnam, later going himself as correspondent for *Newsday*. He died in 1968, a man who had always shown a loving care for the simple, often underprivileged and wayward people about whom so much of his work was written. This commentary on *Of Mice and Men* and *The*

Pearl will, I hope, reveal his main concerns, but I should like to leave this short account of his career with some words of his own which underline the quintessential humanity and humility of the man. Always the love of Malory and of *Morte D'Arthur* was there; as he wrote to Douglas Fairbanks jun, 'For at least 35 years and maybe longer – I have been submerged in research for the timeless *Morte D'Arthur*.' The pull that he felt was deeply sympathetic and intellectual and, in a curious way, spiritual; and I know of no other writer who has seen himself, his role and his achievement with such courageous clarity and self-honesty. Here are his words, from a letter to John Murphy written in 1961:

Nine tenths of a writer's life do not admit of any companion nor friend nor associate. And until one makes peace with loneliness and accepts it as part of the profession, as celibacy is a part of priesthood, until then there are times of dreadful dread. I am just as terrified of my next book as I was of my first. It doesn't get easier. It gets harder and more heartbreaking and finally, it must be that one must accept the failure which is the end of every writer's life no matter what stir he may have made. In himself he must fail as Launcelot failed – for the Grail is not a cup. It's a promise that skips ahead – it's a carrot on a stick and it never fails to draw us on.

Recommended reading

American Literature: selected and introduced by Geoffrey Moore (Faber & Faber 1964).
Tradition and Dream: by Walter Allen (Phoenix House 1964, Penguin Books 1965). This is a very good survey of British and American fiction from the 1920s onwards, with an interesting section on Steinbeck.
Steinbeck: A Life in Letters: edited by Elaine Steinbeck and Robert Wallsten (Heinemann 1975). A must for the Steinbeck enthusiast – more revealing than any biography could be.

Of Mice and Men
Title and background

The title of this story is taken from Robert Burns's famous poem 'To a Mouse, On Turning her up in her nest with the Plough', November 1785. The reference comes in the seventh verse, the last two lines of which read:

> The best laid schemes o' mice an' men
> Gang aft a-gley.

'Often go wrong' is the translation of the last line, and Steinbeck has worked the spirit of the poem, which is humane and compassionate, into the fabric of his story. When Lennie inadvertently kills a mouse, he has wrecked its little life; and when George plans for Lennie to keep out of trouble, his schemes come to nothing because of the huge strength of his companion. Burns's poem identifies man and nature; nothing, however small, is beyond the reach of sympathy and concern. Steinbeck, paradoxically, reverses the emphasis with omniscient irony: nothing is beyond the range of compassion, however big.

There is no political focus in *Of Mice and Men* as there is in *In Dubious Battle* or *The Grapes of Wrath*, though there is a general consciousness of the unsettled economic and social background to the story. References to Soledad and the Salinas river identify the area of California, and we know that Steinbeck worked as a ranch-hand near King City, which is close to Salinas and Monterey. The time appears to be the early thirties – judging from the references to Hollywood and the movies – though it could be in the twenties.

Plot and structure

Of Mice and Men was first published in 1937 and has sold consistently ever since. It has been successfully filmed, and is generally recognized as representing Steinbeck at his economical, evocative, literary and social best. Like *The Pearl* it is a long story, and although it has no numerical chapter sequence, it has divisions which effectively convey the switch in emphasis which movement from one chapter to another so often does. Steinbeck is the master of the short–long story, the tale with a sharpness of direction which precludes investigation at novel length. It is a category which has enjoyed particular esteem in its practice; we think of Maupassant's *Boule de Suif*, Thomas Mann's *Death in Venice*, Somerset Maugham's *Rain* and D. H. Lawrence's *The Fox*, all of which underline how a focus on two or three characters (or sometimes only one) can provide a satisfying artistic and moral expression. The basic plot of *Of Mice and Men* is straightforward, the structure coherent and rounded: two agricultural labourers, bound together by the human need of each other as a fence against insecurity and loneliness, are moved on, or forced to move on, from farm to farm. This is because of the propensity of the one to get into trouble despite the careful planning and the protective attitude of the other. Lennie, giant of a man, simpleton, almost idiot, loves to 'pet' small animals, mice, puppies, anything pretty – a girl's dress, for example, or her hair; he is so strong, however, that other men are as mice to him, for he can kill, as he kills his pets, without any awareness of his own power. George is sane, balanced, the little man who is both big brother and father to the apprehensive and stumbling Lennie. Steinbeck sets the scene beautifully, firmly in nature, with George telling Lennie how to behave when they reach the farm the following day; the scene is at once prologue to the action and epilogue too (for an examination of this, see the section on *Style*).

Both men have their work-cards, obtained in Weed, which they were forced to leave because a girl screamed when Lennie touched her dress; they are going to work at a ranch, but have been put down some miles from it by the bus-driver. They are each, in their respective ways, living on a dream. George, organizer and practical man, keeps Lennie's imagination alive – and his own – by telling of the smallholding they will one day have together when they have raised enough money by working. For George, aware of the wayward and poor life of all their kind, is determined to acquire that 'stake' by fore-going the pleasures of the pool-room and the brothel; for Lennie, it is to be a life of rabbit-tending, petting and the small responsibilities which George will apportion to him. George rehearses him carefully for the following day, knowing that Lennie cannot afford to talk, since talk means revelations, easily misinterpreted, of why he and Lennie have had to move on yet again. He also tells Lennie to hide in the brush, where they are now, should he ever get into trouble. Then they sleep – the break in the text effectively constituting the end of a chapter.

After the break there is the description of the bunkhouse at the ranch; Lennie and George are greeted by an old man – later known as Candy – who has one hand. He tells them of the set-up on the ranch; then the boss enters, still a little angry that they had not turned up the previous day. Lennie, spoken to, nearly gives the game away, but George passes him off as a cousin for whom he is responsible. He also points out what a fine worker he is. Next they meet the boss's son, Curley, a good amateur boxer who has recently married. He sets out to provoke Lennie, but after he has gone George, intuitively anticipating what is to come, warns Lennie about him but at the same time tells him to 'let 'im have it'. Curley's wife in-troduces herself by appearing, provocatively, and, as is her wont, pretending to look for Curley. Then 'the prince of the ranch', the 'jerkline skinner', Slim, introduces himself to them, and bunkhouse life begins; Carlson comes in, then an angry Curley, and this sequence ends with Candy's old dog walking 'lamely in through the open door'. Again we have come to a break in the text, a natural end to an unnumbered chapter.

George and Slim strike up an understanding based on mutual respect and sympathy, and George confides to Slim the truth about Lennie, who is meanwhile fondling a pup. Carlson is urging Candy to shoot his old blind dog, who smells; eventually Carlson, with Slim's authority, takes the dog out in order to shoot it. Here we touch one of those poignant moments in the story, where everyone, but more particularly Candy, is listening for the shot that will put an end to the dog's life. Slim goes out to treat a mule, and Whit tells George about Curley's wife and Curley's jealousy; and how the hands can go to Susy's place (a brothel) if they want a good time. Later George, knowing that Lennie has been fondling some pups, again reverts to their dream of the future, re-telling it, suitably garnished, to Lennie. All this is overheard by Candy, and again the poignancy is evident; he urges them to let him go in with them, for he has saved the money he received in compensation for the loss of his hand. Their exchanges are interrupted by the arrival of Curley and Slim, the latter angry because Curley has suspected him of being with his wife. Now Curley is apologetic, but catches Lennie smiling – ironically at the contemplation of the dream – and sets about him with his fists, reducing Lennie's face to pulp; Lennie, responding to George's 'let 'im have it', crushes Curley's hand. The men manage to get Curley away, and Slim makes him promise that he will say that his hand was caught in a machine. Lennie insists that he meant no harm; George pretends to be severe, but admits that Lennie 'ain't done nothing wrong'. Again we reach the natural break of a chapter.

The next sequence is set in the segregated quarters of Crooks, the negro stable buck. It is Saturday night, the men have gone into town and Lennie, lonely, comes to see Crooks, who initially resents his presence. They talk, and Crooks, who is warped both mentally and physically, tries to undermine Lennie's faith in the absent George and in the dreams of the future. Candy joins them – their mere presence in Crooks's room goes some way towards breaking down the racial difference of which the negro is so acutely aware – and then Curley's wife appears, knowing full well where all the men, including her husband, have gone. She questions them about Curley's injured hand, and then makes it clear to Crooks that she could get him 'strung up on a tree so easy it ain't even funny'. She leaves, George returns, and Crooks is left alone with his liniment. This section ends as it began, with the negro in his silent and lonely contemplation.

The next scene – it is evidence of structural awareness that the episodic nature of the story naturally dovetails into scenes – is in the great hay barn where Lennie, inadvertently, has just killed one of the pups he has been petting. He hides it in the hay, and shortly afterwards Curley's wife appears: Lennie tells her confidingly of their dream and she, embittered, tells him of her fallen hopes of a career in the movies and of her frustrating marriage to Curley. Each needs to talk and not listen, each needs the other there to fill the void of loneliness; but, sadly, there is no communication in their talk. That communication is felt, however, through their appreciation of touch; Lennie strokes the girl's hair, 'musses it', panics when she screams, and breaks her neck. He partly covers her with hay and disappears. She is found, Curley vows revenge, and all the men go in pursuit of Lennie; George, who has stolen Carlson's Luger, suspects that Lennie is hiding in the brush. He gets there before the rest, beguiles him by reciting the dream yet again, and shoots him in the back of the head. When the men arrive, it is Slim who understands what motivated George, both in his protection of Lennie and in the humanity

and compassion which made him kill. This may sound para-
doxical, but Steinbeck leaves us in no doubt that George has
considered the alternative: Lennie would have been put away,
perhaps maltreated, mislabelled as a criminal when in fact his
strength, too great for his own gentleness, and his simple need
to express affection have led to death.

The shape, the structure of *Of Mice and Men*, is evident. The
setting of scene, with minute and imaginative natural observation, gives way to the arrival of people, in the shape of George
and Lennie. The minute observation is now of human nature
in response and interaction, and the next step is a movement
into the social situation – the bunkhouse and work on the
ranch – with an exposure of the personal aspects of relation-
ships where space and numbers are confined. Steinbeck is
adept at delineating the group, and more particularly the
sharp interchanges between two or three people at most; as
when Curley assaults Lennie; Lennie visits Crooks; George
talks to Lennie or to Slim; and, superbly, in the conversation
before Lennie kills Curley's wife. As we have noted in the
summary, the full cycle of events ends where it began, by the
pool of the Salinas river.

There is a fine and illuminating economy about the writing
and the shape it takes. The time span of the story – how long
are George and Lennie at the ranch, for example? – is unim-
portant. The focus is on incident: the theme is redolent of loneliness and insecurity and the need for human companionship,
and encompasses the physical, mental and emotional differences between man and man. Deviations from the norm are
commonplace: Lennie is simple and physically grotesque;
Candy has been deprived of a hand; Crooks, aptly named, has
a crooked spine; Curley is obsessed and fidgety, with a chip on
his shoulder. But just as the living is simple, so too are the differences and the emotions. The story moves succinctly to its
inevitable conclusion; and man must be sustained by a dream,
however impossible of fulfilment the dream. Life is hard, and

there is no provision for those who are diffcrent or deprived mentally or physically. For George the result is tragic; and his humane comments are implicit in the simple unravelling of the tale, which never lacks dramatic tension.

Style

The style in *Of Mice and Men* reflects at once a high level of literary art and an acute awareness of places and people, heightened by that treatment of the subject which marks the humanitarian concerned to explore the moral areas of life, perhaps what George Eliot called 'the medium in which a character moves'. Steinbeck is superbly the creator of atmosphere, and always he dwells on nature and the natural background as the 'medium' of his characters. Nature is seen minutely, both factually and imaginatively; it is at once the stage and the scenery for the life drama which is being presented. The opening of this short novel exemplifies this, for Steinbeck knows and lives his nature. The description is limpid with nostalgia, as the author returns to the known place (where hobos 'jungle-up') in imagination and re-creates it for us with the deft touch and the appreciative eye that loves what it knows. Here the tone is simple:

There is a path through the willows and among the sycamores, a path beaten hard by boys coming down from the ranches to swim in the deep pool, and beaten hard by tramps who come wearily down from the highway in the evening ... (p.7)

This immediacy is reinforced by associative touches that are close to poetry: the sycamores have 'mottled, white, recumbent limbs', the 'rabbits sat as quietly as little grey, sculptured stones', a heron is 'stilted' and a lizard 'makes a great skittering'. Steinbeck's description, as you will see from the above, is figurative and evocative; similes, metaphors, onomatopoeia and personifications abound: simple, effective, economically set down, with eye and ear attuned to a fine harmony of expression. The closeness of man to nature is emphasized in *Of Mice and Men*, so that Lennie, who is 'animal', perhaps primitive in innocence, is seen frequently as a bear or a dog, the imagery stressing the simple responses of his nature. The story begins near the deep green pool of the Salinas river, and ends there as well. When Lennie returns to the brush after killing Curley's wife, the same detailed description of the scene is given, with phrases echoing back to that peaceful opening. But this time the description is weighted with symbolic association, association that leads us back to Lennie's terrible, unmotivated violence:

A water-snake glided smoothly up the pool, twisting its periscope head from side to side; and it swam the length of the pool and came to the legs of a motionless hern that stood in the shallows. A silent head and beak lanced down and plucked it out by the head, and the beak swallowed the little snake while its tail waved frantically. (p.88)

Thus nature and the suddenness of killing, a killing that approximates to Lennie's actions, where unifying descriptions and images appear, too; when Lennie crushes Curley's hand, we are told that Curley was 'flopping like a fish on a line'; while he breaks the neck of Curley's wife 'her body flopped like a fish', both descriptions conveying helplessness in the grip of brute strength. The natural cycle is reflected in the primitive repetition of instinct, but both owe their impact on our consciousness to literary art, the telling judgement which successfully sets up associations in our minds.

The consistent use of animal imagery is only one aspect of

Steinbeck's conscious art; a single shot kills Candy's dog, who has outlived its usefulness in the society of man, and a single shot from the same gun kills Lennie, for whom there is no place in that society. This is given a further compassionate extension when we look closely at Steinbeck's language. Here is the old dog before its death:

After a moment the ancient dog walked lamely in through the open door. He gazed about with mild, half-blind eyes. (p.37)

Later there is a description of Candy as he stands in the doorway of Crooks's room, 'scratching his bald wrist and looking blindly into the lighted room' (p.68). Both descriptions spell out the piteous nullity and helplessness of old age, and both are imbued with the author's compassion. For the most part, the 20th-century writer does not use his own voice in his fiction; what he does is to make his own comments through situation and character, and although Steinbeck does this he does much more. He interlaces his narration with wise appraisal, social concern and moral awareness. This aspect of his style – his capacity to speak in his own voice – is nowhere more apparent than in his description of Crooks. He says of the latter that he 'had retired into the terrible protective dignity of the negro', a phrase which shows a thorough and compassionate understanding of the racial underdog who is underprivileged, impotent and knows it. These moments are rare, but they reinforce the sympathetic tone and identify the writer behind the creatures he creates. Sometimes these interjections into the narrative have a mystical flavour, evoking experiences which we apprehend but cannot easily name; such an instance occurs after the killing of Curley's wife:

As happens sometimes, a moment settled and hovered and remained for much more than a moment. And sound stopped and movement stopped for much, much more than a moment. (p.83)

This statement transcends the simple time-scale of the action, and gives point and significance to change; time does go on, just as the story goes on, but all of us, I suspect, carry in our memories moments of still time, charged with meaning for us alone.

Steinbeck, as I have indicated, uses language symbolically. Not only is the natural background the beginning and the end, the full circle of the action, but the effect of light, the natural light of the sun and the artificial light of the interiors, is an important facet of Steinbeck's unvoiced commentary. The action begins on the evening of a hot day, continues with George and Lennie talking in darkness and half-darkness, with the fire lighting the trunks of the trees until the 'sphere of light' from the fire grows smaller. The next day they go to the ranch-house, and we are told that at 10 o'clock in the morning 'the sun threw a bright, dust-laden bar through one of the side windows, and in and out of the beam flies shot like rushing stars'.

The language is particularly significant; 'stars' recalls night although it is day, and establishes at once the permanence of the cosmic cycle and the inevitability of everything; whether, so to speak, outside or inside man. The mention of 'dust' and 'flies', both symbolic of dirt and disease, represents the degraded way of life of the men living in the bunkhouse. But at least it is natural light, although 'the flies whipped through it like sparks'; when that light is blotted out, it signifies a threat even to this sordid security, and our first sight of Curley's wife is somewhat dimmed, for 'the rectangle of sunshine in the doorway was cut off. A girl was standing there looking in'. Evening in the bunkhouse is lit by the 'tin-shaded electric light', its artificial beams reflecting the artificiality of the life led by the men, with their pulp magazines, their cards, their talk and their encroachments one on the other. All the talk between George, Lennie and Candy takes place with this light for background, almost as if their dream too provides an artificial form of sustenance. In Crooks's lonely room, symbol of his separateness, 'a small electric globe threw a meagre yellow light' which, pathetically, Lennie sees, and which moves him to say 'I thought I could jus' come in an' set'. Here even Crooks, after a while, responds to the dream told in Lennie's excited, childlike way, though his inherent cynicism urges him to reject it.

The light in the barn is also given a considered stress when Lennie first tries to bury the puppy and then kills Curley's wife. A fine atmosphere, illusory as a dream or as if nothing has happened, informs the description here:

The sun-streaks were high on the wall by now, and the light was growing soft in the barn. Curley's wife lay on her back, and she was half covered with hay. (p.81)

When Lennie returns to the brush and the pool, we see his coming death signalled by the description, but the temporary irradiation also indicates George's capacity to perform a humane action in a sad world:

The light climbed on out of the valley, and as it went, the tops of the mountains seemed to blaze with increasing brightness. (p.89)

It invests the scene with that aura of moral and spiritual decision attainable by the humble, whose lives are otherwise poor and frustrated. And then, just before George shoots Lennie, we are told, 'The shadow in the valley was bluer, and the evening came fast', while Lennie looks up 'the darkening slopes of the Gabilans'. There is no more light; but the consonance between Steinbeck's running description and the mood or, more particularly, the situations of his characters, shows that light and life, darkness and death, are indelibly related in his mind.

Much of the foregoing might be called the poetic element in Steinbeck's style; it is consummately balanced by the uncompromising realism of the language his characters use. Steinbeck's method is essentially simple and direct at all times;

he sets a scene, describes a situation, either in jewelled metaphors or the practical language of fact. Crooks's room, the bunkhouse, the individual characters, the horses in the stables, Curley's wife, are all seen with the searching and wise eyes of truth and experience. The language can be as commonplace as the setting:

And these shelves were loaded with little articles, soap and talcum powder, razors and those Western magazines ranch-men love to read and scoff at and secretly believe. (p.20)

But sometimes the tone is lyrical, perhaps idealized, for in the main Steinbeck's people are what John Bayley has called, in another context, 'the characters of love'. Here is Slim:

His ear heard more than was said to him, and his slow speech had overtones not of thought, but of understanding beyond thought. His hands, large and lean, were as delicate in their action as those of a temple dancer. (p.34)

Set against these descriptions is the spoken communication of the characters – colloquial, direct, ungrammatical, slangy but always redolent of truth; there is no difficulty in bringing Steinbeck to the cinema or television screen or into the theatre, since his dialogue translates from the page to the dramatic action with ease and naturalness. His ear rightly tells him to trust his memory; Lennie is characterized through his speech, as are George, Slim, Curley and Candy and, of course, the crippled Crooks. The slang coinages of the time abound – 'bum-steer', 'jail-bait', 'stake', 'rat-trap', 'take the rap' – together with the commonplaces of the semi-literate ('brang a gallon of whisky') and the consistent misuse of 'they' for 'their' and 'of' for 'have'. The language of Curley's wife is particularly apposite and reflects the era, with the cheap glamour of 'shows' and the idea of being a 'star' in Hollywood:

'Coulda been in the movies, an' had nice clothes – all of them nice clothes like they wear. An' I coulda sat in them big hotels, an' had pitchers took of me.' (p.79)

Only once in *Of Mice and Men* does Steinbeck's certainty of touch fail him, and that is when Lennie, alone in the brush and waiting for George, has a visitation:

And then from out of Lennie's head there came a little fat old woman. She wore thick bull's-eye glasses and she wore a huge gingham apron with pockets, and she was starched and clean. She stood in front of Lennie and put her hands on her hips, and she frowned disapprovingly at him.

And when she spoke, it was in Lennie's voice ... (p.89)

It is a laudable attempt to verbalize Lennie's thoughts, but the overall effect is unconvincing, as if a cartoon character has been introduced into a real-life situation; for a moment we are in Disneyland.

It is the novel's only blemish. In truth to life through idiom and usage, at least in this story, Steinbeck is supreme; his ear never fails him and this, with his lyrical, symbolic, factual and figurative modes, makes him a writer who can be appreciated at once on an aesthetic and a humanitarian level. *Of Mice and Men*, despite its sombre content, transcends its time by the simple expedient of being true to that time; there is tragedy in life, just as there is in poetry, and there is the romance of the dream in all its pathetic modesty, and the reality of the horse-shoe game, bunkhouse and cat-house with their little escapes from the hard work, loneliness and deprivation which is the lot of the itinerant ranch-hand. The overall characteristic of Steinbeck's style is its superb economy, whether in word-painting or dialogue, so that nature is seen clearly and imaginatively, and man is appraised truthfully and without distortion.

The characters

Strictly speaking, George and Lennie dominate the action, but it is no mean tribute to Steinbeck's ability that, in a story of this length, he is able to create, almost at the stroke of a pen, convincing, lifelike people. Admittedly, there is, on occasion, an edge of caricature inevitable when there is little space for psychological preparation, but always the outlines are credible. Perhaps the reason lies in the fact that Steinbeck realizes an essential truth, namely that many people *are* types rather than individuals, and that they live in the dimension of their obsessions and dreams when fulfilment and the chance to become more complete are denied them.

George

'Guys like us, that work on ranches, are the loneliest guys in the world. They got no family. They don't belong no place. They come to a ranch an' work up a stake, and then they go inta town and blow their stake, and the first thing you know they're poundin' their tail on some other ranch. They ain't got nothing to look ahead to.' (p.17)

The above quotation symbolizes George, and George in his turn symbolizes a way of life, a kind of nomadic existence from ranch to ranch and bunkhouse to bunkhouse, bucking grain, never having anything to call his own, obstinately clinging to a dream, the impossibility of which he realizes himself in his saner moments. He is the hero, perhaps with Slim, of the story, inherently good and right-thinking, but without the economic means to do anything about his position. Although he tries to protect Lennie, he himself needs Lennie very badly, for his major fear, like Lennie's, is the fear of loneliness. He is sensible and loyal, loyal to Lennie because he knows that he is

a giant innocent, yet his attitude outwardly is one of indigna-
tion, general rebellion, and the much-advertised feeling of
being long-suffering. He tells Lennie, 'When I think of the
swell time I could have without you, I go nuts. I never get
no peace'. But this grumbling conceals an infinitely soft in-
terior. He continues to tell Lennie of their dream (as Lennie
says, 'It ain't the same if I tell it'), plans carefully how to
keep Lennie out of trouble (by getting him not to talk), and
takes a long look into the future by working out how to save
him if he does do something 'bad'. George's outward aggression, which springs from insecurity, the lack of a 'home', is
revealed when they are being shown the bunkhouse by Candy.
We are told that George is 'working up a slow anger', and
this characteristic is reflected in another character who has
no possessions, Carlson, who works up his own anger against
the smell of Candy's dog and eventually gets Slim's permis-
sion to shoot it.

During the interview with the boss George keeps his head
admirably, explaining their reasons for leaving their previous
work, and almost succeeding in keeping Lennie's mouth shut.
The boss is suspicious of George, considering him a 'wise guy'
and failing to understand his bond of sympathy with Lennie.
George is astute at summing people up, sensing at once the
danger of Curley ('I don't like mean little guys'); at the same
time he enjoys (in a secret way) the fact that if Curley does
become too cocky Lennie will deal with him at his (George's)
instigation. He also recognizes Slim not merely as the 'prince
of the ranch' in terms of his working skills, but also in terms
of his humanity and integrity; George's own humanity emer-
ges in his treatment of Candy, firstly when he takes a sympathetic interest in the old man's dog and later when he
virtually admits the swamper to a share in the dream. He is
superstitious, contemplating his solitaire lay, seeing trouble in
the cards and suspecting that it will emanate from Curley;
he is suspicious, too, when Curley's wife comes ostensibly in

search of her husband, sensing that he will have trouble with Lennie over her.

George has a strong awareness, almost bordering on clairvoyance, of the possibilities inherent in a situation, and as self-appointed mentor to Lennie he carries this super-awareness always with him. He has to think and plan for them both, and the responsibility has a constant accompanying tension. But George's simple feelings have deep roots, as we see when he tells Slim of the time that he asked Lennie to jump into the Sacramento River although he couldn't swim a stroke. What happened is part of George's moral education, and demonstrates that his relationship with Lennie is not one-sided: George has come to appreciate the fundamental decency of Lennie's nature:

'He damn near drowned before we could get him. An' he was so damn nice to me for pullin' him out. Clean forgot I told him to jump in. Well, I ain't done nothing like that no more.'

This indicates a capacity for moral growth in George, a capacity which is perhaps exemplified by his killing of Lennie. The latter action is subject to the conventional strictures of morality and the law (how cleverly Steinbeck cuts off the narrative before the ramifications of George's action can be felt). The law would condemn both Lennie and George, for it is not concerned with a humane understanding of man's actions, but only with the results. It is one of Steinbeck's most positive attributes that he should place his own sympathy, his own humanity, so incontrovertibly on the side of the man who has shown *his* humanity in a time of unparalleled crisis; this is a deliberate if unvoiced commentary on George's nature, for George is, one feels, his author's mouthpiece, the moral pivot of the action.

Yet George has moments of sublime pathos, particularly when his own dream takes hold of him, and he is overcome by the prospects of his own vision. When Candy is drawn into it too, George becomes possessive about the dream, warning him not to tell anyone about it, guarding his own secret as if he is ashamed of the sentiment that has caused him to indulge it. The acid, terrible test of George's character comes with the discovery of Curley's wife dead in the barn where Lennie has left her. Practicality, compassion, knowledge of the world, are all to be found in his reaction:

'I guess we gotta get 'im an' lock 'im up. We can't let 'im get away. Why, the poor bastard'd starve.'

He tries to reassure himself – 'Maybe they'll lock 'im up an' be nice to 'im' – but George knows the way of the world too well. The moment of decision, of assured responsibility, is his, and he does not shirk it. He tells old Candy exactly how to act, gets Carlson's Luger while pretending that Lennie has stolen it, seeks Lennie out in the bush and relates the dream yet again, keeps his own head and shoots him, moved by compassion and necessity. We sense, in that terrible moment, and another kind of death, the death of something within George himself; he is once more alone, and it is difficult to sustain your dreams when you have no one to tell them to. For Lennie was George's focus of love, complaint, need; and by killing him he is loyal, both to himself and Lennie, for life without that dream would not be worth living to Lennie, and the greater part of George's tragedy is that he has to live on.

Lennie

. . . a huge man, shapeless of face, with large, pale eyes, with wide, sloping shoulders; and he walked heavily, dragging his feet a little, the way a bear drags his paws. His arms did not swing at his sides, but hung loosely and only moved because the heavy hands were pendula. (p.8)

The above description is our first sight of Lennie, the large, cumbersome, blundering, simple, often inarticulate man whose physical strength and the need to pet something soft and 'purty' are the cause of so much trouble to himself and George. That he is simple-minded is unquestionable; in today's jargon, we should probably call him 'retarded'. His language, when he speaks, is essentially simple and repetitive, like that of a child, and it is this childlike attitude towards the mouse, the pups, the dream rabbits and even Curley's wife's hair which places him beyond condemnation. He has the impress of innocence, his real happiness coming when he listens, as a child would, to the fairy-story of George's plan for their future. Not only are we made aware initially of that colossal size; we find that Lennie is presented in terms of a series of running animal associations. He is seen, for example, as a bear and as a domestic dog, yet such is Steinbeck's method that these associations enhance rather than undermine his innocence; for animals, inarticulate like Lennie, have their own instinctive beings which are innocent of the sophistications of man.

Lennie has no discrimination, drinks water regardless of whether it is bad or not, wants ketchup with his beans, craves stories from George despite the latter's tiredness, forgets that George has his work-card, and sacrosanctly guards his dead mouse until George removes it. He is always vulnerable; has a certain cunning in concealment (the cunning of a disobedient child perhaps); and, despite his windswept memory and inability to concentrate, a certain capacity to play his cards right with George. He threatens to go to a cave, to leave and fend for himself, knowing full well that George will put an end to this talk, albeit with flamboyant severity of tongue, by reverting to the vision of their joint future. Typical of this childlike cunning is the statement:

'If you don't want me, you only jus' got to say so, and I'll go off in those hills right there – right up in those hills and live by myself. An' I won't get no mice stole from me.' (p.17)

Here Steinbeck himself is cunning, indicating not only Lennie's transparent simplicity but also his fate – the fact that he has to flee, in the end, like an animal and, of course, that he is shot like one, like a dog that has gone mad and savaged its victim. As George so poignantly puts it, 'Jesus Christ, somebody'd shoot you like a coyote if you was by yourself.'

Lennie is the central pathetic image in the story, seen always with compassion and understanding by the author, by George and, because of his wisdom, by Slim. Without provoking Curley, he is beaten about the face and crushes Curley's hand when George shouts to him, but we remember his own cry of terror and his plea to George to 'Make 'um let me alone', and his reaction as he 'watched in terror the flopping little man whom he held'. Lennie's lack of coordination, his inability to harness his great strength to any balanced response, means that he is liable to panic, that he is rough when he means to be gentle, that he kills when he means to caress. If George is Steinbeck's moral and social mouthpiece, then Lennie shows the triumph of his humanitarian concern. There is a certain courage too in his portrayal of Lennie, for what Lennie symbolizes is not merely his own mental and emotional inadequacy, but that of society too. And it is a sobering thought that, nearly forty years on from this story, that inadequacy still exists.

Other characters

For the most part, real though these are, they are not treated in depth, and what I intend to do in this brief section is to indicate outlines only, saying more what they represent rather than what they are. The interested student will test the quality of Steinbeck's portrayal – say of Slim, Crooks and Candy – by digging a little deeper psychologically.

Slim is the 'prince of the ranch', the 'jerkline skinner', wise, humane, taking decisions in his stride, authorizing Carlson to shoot Candy's dog, perhaps realizing that discontent in the bunkhouse is the surest way to trouble. He understands George's affinity with Lennie, sees to one of his injured mules, is angry but contained when Curley suspects him of seeing his wife, and is treated by Steinbeck in a somewhat idealized manner; he is the judge, the arbiter, holding the balance between right and wrong. It is Slim who tells Curley to say that he got his hand caught in a machine, and it is Slim who conveys, though his words are few, his understanding and acceptance of George's shooting Lennie – 'You hadda, George. I swear you hadda. Come on with me.'

Candy represents the extreme from Slim – he is maimed, old, useless except as swamper in the bunkhouse, pathetic in the extreme, wishing to be shot (as his dog is) when he has no value to anyone. He catches on to the dream, makes himself a part of it; the theme of loneliness, which runs throughout the story, is written in every reaction of Candy's. He clings to his old dog as George and Lennie cling to one another, and turns his face away when it is shot; his pleas for its life have been moving enough. With the killing of Curley's wife he sees the end of the dream, and there is no more poignant moment in the narrative than his abject realization of it:

He snivelled, and his voice shook. 'I could of hoed in the garden and washed dishes for them guys.' He paused, and then went on in a sing-song. And he repeated the old words: 'If they was a circus or a baseball game ... we would of went to her ... jus' said "ta hell with work", an' went to her. Never ast nobody's say so.' (p.85)

Crooks is a fascinating brief study, only appearing in the story two-thirds of the way through. As the negro stable buck he has a separate room which he, and the white ranch-hands (but not Lennie) regard as private. But he too is lonely, using liniment on his work-worn limbs to ease the physical pain; but the mental pain is too deep-rooted to be erased. He is separate because of his colour, he is inferior because of his colour, he is different because of his colour, the underprivileged outsider in a small white society. He never forgets it, except when he stands up to Curley's wife and is put in his place so severely by her that he reverts to the abject negro slave, in humiliation and fear of the consequences. He resents Lennie's visit, but gradually comes round because of his own human need for companionship; he snipes at Lennie's faith in George, perhaps an expression of his warped view of life, and mocks at the dream, having heard the story before from so many itinerants, none of whom succeeded in saving the money to get the small-holding they wanted. Again, Steinbeck's compassion is evident; Crooks is intelligent but has no outlet for his abilities, being constricted because of his race and his physique.

Curley is the son of the boss, a man small in mind and body, but thought to be a Golden Gloves champion and hence dangerous; he is aggressive, has 'ants in his pants', and constantly seeks to impose his will on others by a demonstration of his prowess. He meets his match in Slim, has his hand crushed by Lennie after he has punched him, and leads the search party for Lennie at the end, swearing that he will shoot him in the guts – 'That'll double 'im over'. He married his wife suddenly, has an overriding jealousy of her – he knows her tendencies – but goes to the cat-house on Saturday night with the rest of the boys. He cannot be 'canned' since he is the boss's son; he appears to be a loose-living character, though he does agree not to say anything about Lennie breaking his hand.

Curley's wife hates him. She is called a tart, and acts like one, appearing in the bunkhouse whenever possible, giving everyone the 'eye', always with the excuse that she is looking for Curley. But in her the theme of loneliness again becomes apparent; she had wanted a life of 'shows' and 'pitchers' and ends up as the only woman on a ranch, with a husband who watches her every move. Her conversation (if it can be called that) with Lennie is a recital of her grievances and her lost hopes and, tinsel though they are, we cannot help but recognize her need for love, not lust, for warmth, not show. She is cheap, seductive, pathetic and, ironically, death restores to her face the girlhood she had lost in her life.

Carlson is a ranch-hand who objects to the smell of Candy's dog, which he shoots. He seems to accept Slim's word as law, and does not emerge as a positive character.

Whit seems to be intent on what he thinks is good-living, going down to the cat-house on Saturdays, and reading pulp magazines and playing cards in the bunkhouse. Again only the merest description is given, but the outlines, filled in partly in some of these characters, pencilled lightly in others, always have the imprint of truth.

Textual notes

Of Mice and Men has no chapters, and therefore no summaries are included in this section, largely because the plot has been quite fully explored in the earlier section which deals with 'Plot and structure'. Students intent on tracing the plot should refer to this section.

Pages 7–23

Soledad A small town on the Salinas River.

Salinas River The name derives from the Spanish, meaning 'salt marshes'. It flows through what is now a rich agricultural region in California.

Gabilan mountains Range overlooking Soledad.

leaf junctures Steinbeck is greatly interested in all forms of plant and animal life, and here is evidence of his minute natural observation.

mottled, white, recumbent limbs Notice here not only the natural observation, but also the subtle personification which brings nature alive.

skittering Effective onomatopoeic usage which conveys perfectly the *sound* of movement.

'coons i.e. racoons, grey-brown furry carnivorous animals.

split-wedge A reference to the shape of the hooves.

jungle-up American colloquial term meaning a camp for tramps or hobos.

as quietly as little grey, sculptured stones A finely observant simile which conveys the stillness of rabbits, a quality less often remarked on than their movements.

stilted heron A heron, a wading bird, has very long legs and an awkward walking movement as a result.

a bear drags his paws The first of the animal images associated with Lennie, indicating both his ponderousness and his power.

pendula Plural of the more commonly used pendulum, but conveying the automatic, virtually mindless movements of Lennie.

snorting into the water like a horse Simple simile to convey his size and the instinctive way he does things.

of rode clear George speaks colloquially, carelessly: 'of' should be 'have' and 'rode' 'ridden'.

Jes' Just.

work cards Identity evidence for their employer.

A live mouse ... a dead mouse This short dialogue encompasses the title of the story and its moral. Lennie's gentleness is death, he cannot help his strength.

Weed A town in northern California lying well inland, in fact towards the border with Oregon.

That's swell That's good, that's the right idea.

you on my tail With you following me.

A water-snake ... like a little periscope A combination of natural observation and imaginative appraisal. A periscope is the 'eye' of a submarine, which strikes and kills. Ironically, in the final sequence, a water-snake is eaten by a hern (heron).

a little wind that died immediately Fine evocation of a still atmosphere.

thrashin' machines i.e. which separate the grain by beating it out.

bucking grain-bags, bustin' a gut Loading or unloading, passing from one to another, with the risk of injury, particularly to the stomach muscles.

an elaborate pantomime of innocence A carefully chosen phrase by Steinbeck. Pantomimes are simple, larger than life, grotesque, clownish. Lennie is all these, particularly when he is trying to be articulate.

the brush line Underwood, thickets, small trees.

like a terrier who doesn't want to bring a ball to its master The relationship between the two men is virtually established by this image, with George as master, Lennie as faithful dog – but sometimes dangerous.

You always killed 'em An unconsciously ironic anticipation of what Lennie's strength portends.

A big carp rose to the surface Here Steinbeck is working through imaginative association. Carp are large and, like Lennie, they kill.

A dove's wings whistled over the water Minute natural observation with an ironic overtone; the dove represents peace, which is what these men want and are destined not to have.

bindle A bundle containing clothing and, perhaps, cooking utensils.

bucks American dollars.

cat-house Brothel.

set in a pool-room ... shoot pool This is a game played on a billiard table, involving the potting of the balls in a set order. Gambling among the players is frequent.

irrigation ditch i.e. a ditch dug to keep the land supplied with water.

put you in a cage with about a million mice and let you have fun George in a temper can speak like this, but he really fears imprisonment for Lennie and what might be done to him, and this is one of the reasons why he shoots him in the end.

I go nuts I go mad.

I'd find a cave In view of the animal associations with Lennie, this is part of the sequence.

coyote North American prairie wolf.

Guys like us ... to look ahead to George's statement is central to an understanding of the story as a whole. There is an underlying pathos in this account of itinerant working man, homeless, spending what money they have aimlessly, and seeing nothing at the end of their working lives.

a stake Deposit, savings. To **blow** it is to spend it.

pounding their tail Working to the point of exhaustion.

blowin' in our jack Spending our money.

Because ... because Even the punctuation and the repetition indicate Lennie's inarticulate manner.

fatta the lan' i.e. to live in comfort or luxury by raising their own crops, etc.

Sacramento Large town in California to the north-east of San Francisco.

yammered Onomatopoeic word conveying the sound of the cry or bark of the coyote.

burlap ticking Coarse canvas covers of bedding.

vials Small vessels used for holding liquid, medicine, etc.

a round stick-like wrist Notice that this story deals with deprivation, particularly of those who are either physically or mentally lacking.

roaches, and other scourges. Cockroaches, and other instruments of vengeance or punishment (like lice or bugs perhaps). The degradation of their situation is being stressed.

pants rabbits Presumably lice or other creatures that breed quickly.

swamper Casual farm labourer.

grey-backs Body lice.

'gimme my time' Pay me the money due to me, because of the time I have worked.

liniment Embrocation, oil used to rub the body to relieve muscular pains, rheumatism, etc.

burned Angry.

the stable buck The negro employed to look after the horses and the stables.

Little skinner ... took after the nigger The driver of six- or eight-horse teams ... took a dislike to.

poop Here it means 'energy', that Candy is too old or exhausted.

Stetson A slouch hat of a type originally worn by Australian/New Zealand soldiers, and affording considerable protection against the sun.

bum steer False, inaccurate information.

grain teams Gangs of men working together, loading.

two buckers Two loaders.

Pages 24–35

Strong as a bull Again the animal image to characterize Lennie, but this time with an ominous overtone.

rassel grain-bags, drive a cultivator i.e. load them, and drive the machine which breaks up the ground and uproots weeds.

put up a four-hundred-pound bale This shows Lennie's strength – he can lift this amount unaided.

'what you sellin'?' What's your game, what are you up to?

cesspool A well sunk in the soil, which retains solids and allows liquids to escape.

flapper Mouth.

drag-footed ... pale, blind old eyes Superb description of age, pathetically linking the dog and its owner, both of whom have little but existence left to them.

ast Ask.

gingerly With extreme caution.

'What the hell's he got on his shoulder?' The equivalent to 'a chip on his shoulder', resentful insecurity, which accounts for his aggression.

He's done quite a bit in the ring He's quite a good boxer.

punk American slang for a worthless, rotten person.

game i.e. like a game-cock, spirited, plucky.

slough To be shed or cast off (like the skin of a snake).

canned Sacked.

fulla vaseline The latter is a substance obtained from petroleum, much used in ointments. The implication is sexual – a hand kept soft for caressing.

solitaire A card game for one player, usually to be equated with the more commonly known 'patience'.

Purty Pretty.

she got the eye She is naturally flirtatious, she encourages anyone.

Curley's pants is full of ants He is constantly restless, fretting.

jerkline This is a single rein fastened to the brake handle that runs through the driver's hand to the bit of the lead animal.

whipped through it like sparks Superbly economical image conveying the sense of movement against the light.

flounced Threw (the cards) together.

set-up The organization, structure (of things here).

sock Hit, punch.

tangles ... get the can Gets involved ... (we'll) get the sack.

plug himself up for a fighter Make a reputation as a boxer

the jingle of trace chains Another onomatopoeic usage, the ropes or chains of the harness.

let 'im have it Use all your strength on him.

Hide in the brush ... down in the brush Not only is this a foreshadowing of what actually happens, it also reinforces the animal images associated with Lennie. He is forced to flee, hide and be trapped, like an animal.

rolled clusters, like sausages Unusual image. Steinbeck is adept at using the commonplace, particularly if its shape or sound is evocative

mules Heel-less slippers.

bouquets of red ostrich feathers Ostentatious adornment, perhaps indicative of her 'tarty' nature.

bridled Expressed offence or awareness by raising her head and drawing in her chin.

'Nobody can't blame a person for lookin' There is a deliberate innuendo here. The girl is ostensibly looking for Curley, but inwardly gratified that the men are looking at her, appraising her sexuality.

jail-bait i.e. the kind of girl who would get a man into trouble. Ironically she does.

take the rap Pay the penalty.

I bet he's eatin' raw eggs i.e. to increase his virility and fitness.

two bits Slang for 25 cents (also called 'a quarter').

a few dollars in the poke i.e. saved up.

the American River In California, near Lake Tahoe.

pan gold To wash sand, gravel, etc, to find gold.

the prince of the ranch Note the dignity with which Steinbeck invests Slim, who is a character seen with loving pride. The humanity behind his presentation is apparent. Steinbeck is saying that in poor groups such as these there are natural leaders as distinct from the privileged rulers. Here it is pride in work which makes for royalty of nature. Slim is a prince in many ways – he is wise, compassionate, understanding and self-disciplined.

the wheeler's butt The flanks of the shaft-horse.

a bull-whip Made of rawhide, with a plaited lash.

hatchet Narrow, sharp.

as those of a temple dancer This invests Slim with a bodily grace and a certain spirituality as well.

brighter'n a bitch It is ironic that Slim should use a commonplace phrase after the author's description of him. He means that it is very hot (like a bitch 'on heat') but there may be a sideways glance at Curley's wife.

slang her pups i.e. gave birth to a litter.

Pages 36–49

Lulu's milk The name of the bitch which had the litter. Her milk would go bad if it were not taken by the surviving pups.

horse-shoe game The throwing of horse-shoes to loop around an upright stake or pole, or some such variant of this, where points are scored.

a cuckoo Someone who is crazy or barmy.

Auburn Town in California north-east of Sacramento.

fence picket A pointed stake used as the upright support.

scairt Scared.

rabbits Talks freely.

scrammed Left hurriedly.

pitch Throw.

Airedale A large rough-coated terrier, named after a place in Yorkshire.

pulp magazine Magazine printed on rough paper, often containing sensational reading or picture material.

whing-ding A spree, a wild, lively thing.

dime's worth 10 cents, the price of the magazine.

Luger Famous make of pistol. The irony lies in the fact that just as the old dog is put out of its misery by Carlson, so the same gun is used by George to put Lennie out of his.

tar Obtained as a liquid by the distillation from wood or coal. It has strong antiseptic properties, hence its use here.

euchre An American card game, for two or four people.

roll up a stake i.e. save some money.

looloo Presumably from Lulu, it means (she) is really worth looking at, she stands out.

yella-jackets Wasps

drawers Underpants.

all set on the trigger The slightest thing will set it off.

set you back? What does it cost you?

two an' a half Two and a half dollars.

a shot for two bits A nip of whisky for 25 cents.

a flop i.e. sexual intercourse, go upstairs with one of the girls.

the joint The place, the establishment.

kewpie-doll A doll in the form of a chubby winged baby with a topknot of hair.

Pages 50–70

phonograph Record-player.

burned Catching a disease.

a crack The equivalent of 'flop'.

goo-goos The initials of 'good government', hence those bent on reform.

Golden Gloves Amateur boxing tournament, begun in 1928 as an inter-city competition between Chicago and New York.

Champions received a gold medal and a diamond-studded trophy.

hoosegow Prison, guardhouse.

San Quentin Maximum security prison in California.

'cots Apricots.

alfalfa Lucerne, a clover-like plant used for fodder.

smoke-house A building where meat or fish is cured by dense smoke.

Jap cook Japanese, with the implication that cheap labour is hired in the ranch-houses.

bunkhouses Communal sleeping quarters for the hands working on a ranch.

does ... litter i.e. the rabbits would breed at regular intervals.

raptly Absorbed by his own vision.

kick-off Die.

swing her Persuade her to accept (the offer).

put me on the county On charity relief payments.

was popped into the future The whole of this exchange is pathetic. The present is so bad that their minds 'pop' into the dream that cushions reality.

squack The onomatopoeic affect conveys immediate decision.

to bind her To keep her to the agreement, make her honour it.

yella as a frog belly i.e. you're a coward.

welter A weight in boxing, 66 kg (10½ stone).

huge paws ... bleated The animal associations, with bear and sheep, express the contradiction in Lennie – his strength and his fear.

flopping like a fish on a line The image indicates helplessness and the fact that there is no escape. The same image is used of Curley's wife when Lennie breaks her neck.

buggy Light vehicle, carriage, for use of one or two people.

lit intil Attacked.

hame Piece of curved wood or metal forming part of the collar of a draught horse.

California civil code for 1905 The laws of the county, ironically out of date. Crooks would be acutely aware of his own rights, or lack of them in practice.

crazy as a wedge Crazy.

nail-keg A small barrel.

blabbin' Telling tales, talking too much.

screwy Mad, insane.

he took a powder He just left.

booby hatch The asylum (for the insane).

with a collar, like a dog Ironically Crooks unbeknown to himself, voices George's fear of what could happen to Lennie.

rummy A simple card game played with two packs.

to conceal his pleasure with anger This is poignant, pathetic. Crooks is hungry for companionship, but is forced by his separateness to conceal it.

And a manure pile under the window Heavy irony. The black man's comfort is not considered – he will be put where he is wanted.

take you out in a box i.e. remove you in a coffin.

land in his head i.e. the idea of buying land to farm for themselves.

blackjack A card game in which any player can become the dealer.

to get something on you Find out something that can be used against you.

Pages 71–95

two-by-four Presumably two feet by four feet (61 cm by 1.22 m), a deliberate exaggeration of its smallness.

ol' right cross A technical term in boxing, in which the blow is delivered with the arm bent, not straight.

Baloney Rubbish.

cover 'im up Conceal what really happened.

bums Loafers, scroungers.

shows Touring theatrical companies.

pitchers Pictures, the cinema.

stiffs Tramps.

dum-dum One who is incapable of speaking. She means Lennie, of course.

ol' sheep She is referring to Candy.

terrible protective dignity of the negro A superb phrase to convey the withdrawal into himself of the man who is used to insult through no fault of his own.

floosy Attractive girl of loose morals.

two shots of corn Two nips of whisky.

I might of knew I should have known.

roll your hoop An insulting way of saying that she is childish and ought to be playing childish games.

trap Mouth.

doped out To devise, to work out.

tenement Tournament.

mutt Mongrel dog.

a passion of communication The theme of loneliness is finely stressed in this phrase.

movies The cinema.

Hollywood The home of the motion picture industry in California.

previews The screening of films before the public is generally allowed to see them. Celebrities generally attend them.

a natural i.e. sure to be a success.

made a ringer This is a term generally used in quoits, but here obviously applied to a horseshoe falling round the peg.

muss it up Disarrange it.

her body flopped like a fish See the note on p.35.

And then she was still, for Lennie had broken her neck Superbly, the simple language of understatement, almost as if it is commonplace, and indeed it is a reflex rather than a motivated action.

He pawed up the hay Insistent animal images from now on to convey his state.

She whimpered and cringed to the packing-box Natural animal instinct in the presence of death.

Curley's wife lay ... This whole paragraph is a masterly creation of atmosphere, the peace of what *seems* contrasted with the terrible reality of what *is*.

As happens sometimes, a moment settled ... (See the section on *Style* p.14).

as hard and tight as wood Fine economical image.

lynched Hanged without a trial.

I think I knowed we'd never do her I think I knew we should never get (the place we talked of).

we would of went to her We could have gone to see it (the circus or the game).

a motionless hern Another name for heron.

lanced down Notice that here is death in nature, the moment of killing, as thoughtless, mindless, as Lennie's killing of the girl.

as a creeping bear moves We have returned here to one of the first images used to characterize Lennie.

from out of Lennie's head This achieves a cartoon-like effect.

bull's eye glasses These are like white glass with a dark centre, and seem to add to the distortion and caricature effect.

gingham Cotton or linen cloth of dyed yarn.

snooker Game with various coloured balls of different points value, played on a billiard table.

stew the b'Jesus outa George i.e. take advantage of George.

jack you outa the sewer Keep you from getting into serious trouble.

fambly Family.

blow it in Spend it all.

snapped off the safety Lifted the safety catch (so that it was ready to fire).

is eatin' them two guys? What are those two so upset about?

Revision questions

1 Give an account of the characters of George and Lennie as they are revealed in the first scene by the pool.

2 Indicate, by close reference to the text, Steinbeck's ability to create atmosphere.

3 For which character in the story have you the most

sympathy? Give reasons for your answer, and refer closely to the text in support of it.

4 In what ways is Steinbeck's style in *Of Mice and Men* poetic? You should quote passages in illustration, and comment on them.

5 Show the importance of *any two* of the following in the action of the story: (a) Curley; (b) Curley's wife; (c) Slim; (d) Candy.

6 Write an essay on Steinbeck's use of dialogue in this story, and say what effects he achieves by the use of colloquialisms and slang.

7 Write an essay in appreciation of Steinbeck's use of image and symbol.

8 Write an account of what you consider are the pathetic elements in *Of Mice and Men*.

9 What do you consider to be the main themes in *Of Mice and Men*?

10 In what ways do you detect the presence of the author in the story?

11 How far is Steinbeck successful in conveying the 'medium' in which a character moves?

12 Write an account of any *two* dramatic scenes in *Of Mice and Men*, saying exactly how Steinbeck achieves his effects.

13 What aspects of this story do you find unreal, sentimental or overdone? You should give reasons for your answer.

14 Write an account of Steinbeck's presentation of the relationship between man and nature.

15 Is *Of Mice and Men* pessimistic or optimistic in the main? Refer to the text, and give reasons for your answer.

The Pearl
Origin, plot, background and theme

The story of *The Pearl* is adapted from that indicated by Steinbeck in *The Log from the Sea of Cortez* (published in paperback by Pan Books). Briefly, he tells of how an Indian boy found a pearl of great size, knew that he need never work again if he sold it, and that he could have a good time here on earth and at the same time make advance purchase of Church masses sufficient to set him up in Heaven too. He took it to La Paz, and went from broker to broker, being offered low prices. He realized that he was being cheated, and that they were 'only the many hands of one head'. He hid his pearl, but was attacked, tortured and beaten on successive occasions; finally he crept back to the beach where he had hidden it, took it, threw it into the sea, and became a free man again. Later 'he laughed a great deal about it'. Steinbeck's own comment in *The Log from the Sea of Cortez* is illuminating:

This seems to be a true story, but it is so much like a parable that it can't be. This Indian boy is too heroic, too wise. He knows too much and acts on his knowledge. In every way, he goes contrary to human direction. The story is probably true, but we don't believe it; it is far too reasonable to be true.

Steinbeck gave the Indian boy a wife and child, introduced realism into the parable, and interfused metaphorical and moral comment into his own narrative, but he retained the essential outline.

The *plot* is straightforward. Kino, an Indian fisherman, married, with a child, sees that child stung by a scorpion. At his wife's insistence, Kino tries to get the European doctor to treat his son. The doctor, however, is not interested in curing 'insect bites for "little Indians"'. The next day Kino dives and finds a pearl of great size. Immediately the news spreads; first the priest visits Kino; then the doctor arrives, to fake a temporary sickness in the child so that he can return and supposedly cure it. That night someone tries to steal the pearl, but Kino keeps it, and the following day takes it to the pearl buyers, who have heard the news and agreed between them to offer a low price. Kino is angered and keeps the pearl, for he sees visions of a fine future in it. Again attempts are made to steal it, and Juana urges him to throw it back into the sea. He refuses, but she steals out when he is asleep and is about to throw it when Kino comes after her and beats her. Then he himself is attacked, and kills a man in the struggle. Juana retrieves the pearl, gets the baby but, when Kino approaches his house, he sees that it is alight. He, Juana and the baby shelter in the house of Juan Tomás, letting everyone think that they have perished in the fire, and then they set out, taking the pearl with them in the hope of selling it. They make a long journey into the mountains but are followed by trackers. In desperation Kino decides to attack these men at night, but as he does so one of them fires at a noise which could be made either by a baby or a dog, and kills Kino's baby. Kino kills the men, and then he and Juana return to La Paz carrying the body of their child. They throw the pearl back into the sea, where it rejoins its kind.

The *background* is La Paz in Baja (Lower) California, in the peasant, fishing area. It is clearly and poetically described, and the student who wants to investigate this background should read Steinbeck's *The Log from the Sea of Cortez*, which describes a marine expedition in the Gulf of California.

The *theme* of the story is equally clear cut in outline. The promise of wealth is the great corrupting influence in men's lives, and such is human nature that man will resort to the basest actions in order to gain what he covets. Subsidiary to this is the idea that man and nature are interconnected, and

that simplicity, poetry and a sense of moral value exist in
the poor rather than in those who have already been corrupted
by material things.

Style

The textual notes accompanying this commentary frequently
point out the main facets of Steinbeck's style; this section may
therefore be regarded as a general introduction rather than
a detailed examination. The salient characteristic of Steinbeck's style in *The Pearl* is certainly its simplicity. This reflects
his concern to make the style fit the subject, for the story is
a parable; or at least Steinbeck indicates that readers may find
it so. A parable, or allegory – for here they are the same thing
– typifies through its fiction either moral or spiritual relations,
or both; that is to say, its application is general as well as
specific.

Now the language of a parable is usually sufficiently
elevated to make its wider applications clear, and *The Pearl*
is no exception to this rule. In fact the language of the
story is poetic, for Kino's songs represent the impact of tradition and a way of life upon his inheritance. The constant use
of this music enhances the simplicity, for simple people, like
children, often sing instead of talking, which they find difficult. Running together with this inward music is the outward
music of physical description, for *The Pearl* is impregnated
with superb mirage effects; animal (including snake) imagery;
the visions as seen in the pearl itself, and how these change;
minute observations of nature, and, more particularly, the
establishment of atmosphere or mood through description.

Steinbeck always looks closely at nature, and the effects he achieves vary from the broad perspective to the fine, small appraisal. One senses, too, a superb ability to convey moments, experiences of a visual observation, for example, by the variation of stylistic pace; here are two examples:

The dawn came quickly now, a wash, a glow, a lightness, and then an explosion of fire ... (p.8)

Here time is foreshortened to convey the vividness of effect. The next is different in tone and pace:

The ants were busy on the ground, big black ones with shiny bodies, and little dusty quick ants. Kino watched with the detachment of God while a dusty ant frantically tried to escape the sand trap an ant lion had dug for him. (p.9)

The symbolic element is evident in this passage, for Kino is to find himself in the position of the dust ant, and much later in the story he sees the ants overcoming obstacles, in much the same way as the trackers will overcome the obstacle of finding him. There is the additional sense, too, that Kino is as God to the ants, and that Kino is himself an ant in relation to the God or gods of the universe. Thus Steinbeck, by varying his style to encompass the large and the small, establishes a sense of unity between them. This is worked out on all levels of the story; the sky presages a storm, the trees and the wild-life respond, and the storm within man, of lust and greed and violence, continues unabated. The repetition of simple words in order to establish the simplicity of the peasant way of life is paralleled on another level by the repetition of an image to re-emphasize a character trait, while Kino himself thinks in terms of animal associations.

Interspersed throughout the narrative are ironic comments on man and his selfishness and self-indulgence; thus the beggars were 'great experts in financial analysis', while the doctor's idea of 'civilized living' was 'to keep a mistress and eat in restaurants'. Steinbeck is adept, too, at catching the very tone and substance of hypocrisy. Here is one of the pearl-buyers:

His face was fatherly and benign, and his eyes twinkled with friendship. He was a caller of good mornings, a ceremonious shaker of hands, a jolly man who knew all jokes and yet who hovered close to sadness, for in the midst of a laugh he could remember the death of your aunt, and his eyes could become wet with sorrow for your loss. (p.52)

Steinbeck's appraisal is not merely of individuality, but of human nature in the mass, and it is part of his style to characterize the one by a contemplation of the many. Thus the community of La Paz becomes one in its excitement over Kino's finding of the pearl, for this community, like any other, is man writ large:

A town is a thing like a colonial animal. A town has a nervous system and a head and shoulders and feet ... And a town has a whole emotion.

Here one sees the repetition being used with marked effect, for it conveys the actual *repeating* of the news of Kino's find. One o' he finest things about *The Pearl* – and which brings it so close to poetry – is the fact that it is a sustained piece of metaphorical writing, which never cloys because of the width and range of Steinbeck's heightened language. The capacity of man for self-delusion is seen in natural description that stresses the atmosphere of the Gulf, where the moisture is hung 'in shimmering scarves in the air so that the air vibrated and vision was unsubstantial'. This is the mirage of nature, in contrast to the mirage or vision which Kino sees in the pearl, a vision which changes into frightful reality and symbolizes corruption:

He looked into its surface and it was grey and ulcerous. Evil faces peered from it into his eyes, and he saw the light of burning. And in the surface of the pearl he saw the frantic eyes of the man in the pool. And in the surface of the pearl he saw Coyotito lying in the little cave with the top of his head shot away. (p.94)

It will be seen from this that the symbolic and metaphorical elements are important in any appraisal of Steinbeck, and throughout *The Pearl* they are buttressed by an uncompromising morality, which looks closely at human nature and exposes it for what it is. Yet, as ever in Steinbeck, the compassion, the sympathy, the identification, are never submerged by the sordidness of greed, violence and corruption which are the staple elements of his content. Dialogue is sparse in *The Pearl*, which depends for its effect on a sustained poetic flow, but the brief exchanges of tenderness or fear between Kino and Juana, the false language of the dealers, the rather formal talk between Kino and Juan Tomás, all have the stamp of truth. The economy of the tale, despite multiple repetitions of imagery and phrasing, is remarkable. Structurally, it is rather like the community the author describes, with the central nervous system, the nerve-ends and the emotions all interconnected within the metaphorical frame. The tone can be lyrical or cynical, wise or factual, realistic or visionary, but all are inter-related through the language. Steinbeck is singularly unlike Henry James in terms of style, expression and treatment, but one thing he does share with his great compatriot. He has a sense of form or structure which is highly developed, and he believes in what James believed in, namely total relevance. The dramatic tension never drops, and one has only to trace the journey in flight of Kino and Juana to see how it is sustained by a style as bare as the terrain. As Steinbeck says in the brief prologue to the story, 'perhaps everyone takes his own meaning from it and reads his own life into it'. Perhaps we do, but it is consummate literary art that makes such identification and interpretation possible.

The characters

As in *Of Mice and Men*, the action of *The Pearl* is concerned with two characters, Kino and Juana, and all else is subordinated to them and their experiences. But, as Steinbeck says, the story is a parable, and the characterization is rather different as a result. For example, much more of character is presented through the consciousness than through the speech, but it in no way detracts from the realism, since the author has managed to present the consciousness of Kino, for instance, through the terms in which he would think or respond. The effect is unusual, but it is a triumph of literary art and sympathetic identification, for the author succeeds in convincing us of the essential truth of the simple thoughts, reflexes and decisions of a simple man.

Kino

In Kino's head there was a song now, clear and soft, and if he had been able to speak of it, he would have called it the Song of the Family. (p.8)

Kino is central to all the action of *The Pearl*, for he is the individual, complete in himself, who at the same time symbolizes man and all men. He is a fisherman, dependent for his sparse livelihood on his catches and always with an eye for the opportunity of finding a pearl. He has inherited his way of life and the traditional superstitions and folklore of his forebears; he lives close to the earth, with the minimum of possessions, and he knows nothing of the wide world except for hearsay and stories. He and his people have been used and exploited for generations, but he has a close family life, and a community one; and he wants for his child, Coyotito, a better way of life than he himself has had. He does not articulate this; rather his instinct, his intuition, tell him that there is a better world; and that going to school, learning to read, having a rifle with which to protect yourself, are the summits which may be scaled if you have a valuable pearl. Steinbeck describes Kino with great directness and simplicity, the language harmonizing with his nature:

Kino was young and strong and his black hair hung over his brown forehead. His eyes were warm and fierce and bright and his moustache was thin and coarse. (p.9)

This description, particularly 'strong', 'warm' and 'fierce', foreshadows his actions and reactions in the face of adversity. His simple love of family life gives way to ambition when he acquires the pearl. He is strong – consider the attacks on him and his responses, his physical agility and resilience during the journey and more particularly when he attacks the trackers; he is warm, loving his family, wife and child and the simple daily occupations which constitute his security; and he is fierce to fight, defend, obstinately cling to what is his and to his vision. But despite all this he has the inherent suspicion of the underdog, an intuitive appraisal of the evil in human nature, and a determination to stand out against it. Kino, in a sense, and as Juan Tomás points out to him, takes on the establishment, the fixed patterns of his society, and in this way he symbolizes the rebel in all men and the sufferings they must endure. Steinbeck orchestrates Kino's music, for every situation, good or evil, has an insistent melody, or even a mixture and distortion of melody, in Kino's mind. This constitutes a running, subliminal moral commentary on the action, for his music always sounds the note of truth.

Kino is a loving man, capable of great if unvoiced tenderness to Juana; but he is the head of the family and it is he who makes the decisions. Allied to this is his obstinacy, which makes him cling to the pearl when Juana would have thrown it into the sea; and he asserts his power when she takes the pearl, and beats her. But this simple man, who has the animal instinct of self-preservation and a poetry of the soul that is perhaps best defined by the word love, is educated through suffering to a new recognition of himself. When they return to La Paz, carrying the bundle that is Coyotito, we are told that 'they were not walking in single file, Kino ahead and Juana behind, as usual, but side by side', later, 'Kino's hand shook a little, and he turned slowly to Juana and held the pearl out to her'. Both quotations illustrate indeed that 'they had gone through pain and had come out on the other side'. But the words do more than this: they indicate the shared experience of grief, the terrible equality of suffering, which changes life so that nothing is as it was before. In offering Juana the pearl, in walking beside her and not in front of her, Kino is acknowledging his guilt and responsibility for the death of Coyotito; he is admitting the rightness of her thought and accepting her spirit as her own. The Song of the Family may be sad, but it has ennobling chords that strike the sympathetic ear of the reader.

Kino bears the stamp of his subject race, and his reactions are a compound of fear, frustration and anger, as well as the suspicion we have already noted. The visit to the doctor is a case in point, where Kino shows his impetuosity by striking the gate when they are not admitted, though afterwards we are told that 'He looked down in wonder at his split knuckles'. This frustration gives way to hope after the discovery of the pearl, and he says, movingly, 'We will be married – in the church'; and, of course, there are his ambitions for Coyotito, which betoken an awareness of what life could offer. But Kino knows the way of the world, and makes himself 'a hard skin' against it. After the doctor has supposedly treated Coyotito, Kino 'remembers the white powder', and as his awareness of evil grows and he is thrown back on his animal instinct, clusters of animal images qualify his reactions, so that in the end he fights not for the pearl but to protect his family and, tragically, causes his son's death. But before that, the quality of his spirit is apparent. After he has beaten Juana, and after he has seen his house burnt, he stays temporarily with his brother Juan Tomás, but tells him that he does not want to be a 'leprosy' to him, and decides that they must leave. If sophisticated language could define this, we might say that Kino here behaves decently, or that he is considerate; but it is difficult to comment on a being at once so primitive and poetic as Kino, except to say that he is close to nature, part of it; and to add that the loyalties, the ties within nature, are perhaps stronger than those within the societies of man. The interested student will look closely at Steinbeck's presentation of Kino, and will see how far he penetrates his mind and emotions; suffice to say that the overall effect is moving, real, and taut with the quality of his experiences.

Juana

Her face was hard and lined and leathery with fatigue and with the tightness with which she fought fatigue. And her wide eyes stared inwards on herself. She was as remote and as removed as Heaven. (p.93)

Juana is not explored as fully as Kino, but the above quotation illustrates her suffering, a suffering which would have been avoided if she had had her own way about the pearl. Juana is the subordinate wife, but she is not submissive, although she loves her man for what he is – obstinate, wrong-headed and, once, brutal. She is decisive, and in a way one gets the impression that she is 'brighter' than Kino. It is Juana who decides that they will go to the doctor after Coyotito has been stung by the scorpion. As we are told, 'This was Juana's first baby – this was nearly everything there was in Juana's world.' She is practical, and makes the seaweed poultice which will have to suffice, though it hasn't the doctor's 'authority'. In-

itially, she responds to the finding of the pearl as a good
omen, since when they open the 'lip-like' muscle, Coyotito's
swelling disappears. After the doctor's visit, Juana has to
endure the sight of Coyotito's illness, and she tries to 'ward
off the danger' with the Song of the Family and by muttering
'little magics'; for Juana has absorbed the new religion while
still clinging to the efficacy of the old. She is alert, sensing
danger when Kino does at the first attempt to steal the pearl
from their hut. From then on her woman's intuition motivates
her every reaction. She warns Kino of the evil of the pearl
with prophetic insistence – 'It will destroy us all . . . Even our
son'. After the second attack, when she 'wills' Kino not to
leave the hut and he foolishly does so, she pleads with him
to destroy the pearl. Later she takes it, but just as she is about
to throw it back into the sea, he seizes her and beats her.
She feels no anger against him, for 'Although she might be
puzzled by these differences between man and woman, she
knew them and accepted them and needed them.' Her
appraisal of their situation when she realizes that Kino has
killed a man is immediate and sure, and she realizes 'that
the old life was gone for ever'. Her strength of character and
purpose sustains Kino at the lowest ebb of his morale, for
when she reasons with him about what would happen if the
trackers get them, her language is uncompromising:

'Do you think they would let me live? Do you think they
would let the little one here live?' (p.80)

And later we are told 'He looked then for weakness in her
face, for fear or irresolution, and there was none'. And when it
is all over, and the tragedy has been played, Juana's loyalty
and quality of character are still uppermost. She and Kino
are bound more closely together, and he offers her the pearl
but, with typical tenderness and generosity of spirit, she insists
softly that he should be the one to throw it into the sea, know-

ing that this last action will help sustain his manhood under the reaction of guilt.

Other characters

The only other characters of note in *The Pearl* are the doctor and Juan Tomás. The first represents self-indulgence and greed; he is physically repulsive, cares only for money and what it can buy, is unscrupulous and dishonest – witness his 'faking' of Coyotito's illness – and lives in the memory of his life in Paris. He is the European who has no time for the natives; he treats them like animals, unless he can get something out of them, in which case he is suave, persuasive and cunning. We suspect that he has initiated the attacks on Kino. Juan Tomás represents the voice of sanity and good sense: he fears for himself, and he also fears for Kino. He realizes what Kino has done by rejecting the small offers of dealers, and his philosophy is quite simply expressed – better to accept and be swindled, than reject and be hunted.

But the community of the town itself – the 'colonial animal' – is a character, with its miscellaneous peasants and the cunning dealers who serve one god. The predatory images that surround the dealers again show Steinbeck connecting man and nature – but here in its cruellest, most destructive form.

Chapter summaries
and textual notes

'In the town they tell the story of the great pearl ...' For a brief account of the origin of this story, see the section on 'Origin'. p.40.

Chapter 1

Kino, a poor Indian fisherman and pearl-diver, wakes one morning within the security of his family life. But after breakfast, his small son, Coyotito, is stung by a scorpion. Kino and Juana, his wife, decide to take the child to the doctor, a white man who only treats the wealthy; Kino is told that he is out, and crashes his fist against the gate in his anger.

a pale wash of light in the lower sky to the east Throughout this story there is a strong sense of the vastness of nature, and this opening, with its wide perspective as background to the small lives, sets the pattern.

the brush house in the tuna clump Made of brush wood and surrounded by large tropical plants.

a covey of little birds A brood, family or set, approximating to the cluster of families in the huts.

chittered Notice the onomatopoeic effect.

the lightening square The simple use of light, as in *Of Mice and Men*, to signify life.

hanging-box i.e. rather like a hammock, suspended.

to listen to his music ... The songs remained ... but no new songs were added Steinbeck represents Kino as thinking in terms of songs rather than words, a clever way of stressing his native tradition and the inheritance of folklore as distinct from a more sophisticated way of life, perhaps as exemplified by the doctor. It is, so to speak, a stream of emotional consciousness without the addition of developed intelligence or intellect.

the Song of the Family This is Kino's security, a simple, primitive love of what is his and what he is surrounded by. The irony lies in the fact that it is soon to be threatened, and the song is to change to other songs.

the specks of Gulf clouds flame high in the air This time the more vivid impact of light; the Gulf is the Gulf of California.

spears of light A finely economical metaphor, typical of Steinbeck's imaginative writing in this story.

the grinding-stone This would enable Juana to crush the corn before making it into cakes for their simple breakfast.

with the detachment of God A fine way of indicating his
silence and his position as head of the house.

an ant lion These are large insects which dig in the dust and then
wait for their victims – other ants and insects – to fall in, when
they are devoured. Here it is used symbolically. Kino very nearly
becomes the victim of the ant lions – the pearl dealers and those
employed to track him down.

**It was a morning like other mornings and yet perfect
among mornings** The repetition carries within it the
unchangeable monotony of life and yet the exhilaration of
difference. Again, the irony is apparent in view of what is to
happen.

endless variety of interval The variety depended on its pace
and the pauses between words.

the Whole Everything one could wish for. Note the stress on
'safety' and 'warmth'.

bowed and feinted at each other Describes their movements in
a pantomime of a fight.

ruffed out Stood out (referring to the coloured ring of feathers
round the neck).

game chickens Those bred for cock-fighting.

pulque Mexican fermented drink from the sap of the agave.

fiesta Holiday, festivity.

ancient magic ... Hail Mary A combination of folklore and
native tradition on the one hand and Christian prayer on the
other.

lymphatic mound Raised swelling full of fluid.

as cold as the eyes of a lioness The power of this simile lies in
the fact that the lioness is proverbially strong in defence of its
young. Throughout *The Pearl* Kino and Juana are invested with
animal reactions, firstly to show how close to nature and the earth
they are, and secondly to indicate the strength of their feelings.

music of the family ... steely tone A fine change of mood in
music, conveying the threat, the undermining of safety and
warmth.

the rutted path i.e. full of holes and tracks made by carts.

jiggling Wobbling and jerking.

so that they walked on their own shadows An ominous image, perhaps looking forward to the fact that they almost destroy themselves after they get the pearl.

bougainvillaea Tropical plant, large and bright-coloured.

secret gardens ... caged birds A superb transition to a contrasting way of life, that of sophistication and wealth, where nature grows according to man and is imprisoned or contained by him.

blinding plaza The heat of the sun on the market-place or square.

great experts in financial analysis Overt irony, since they saw everyone and could calculate their wealth or lack of it.

what kind of drama might develop (To see) whether there would be an incident or scene. The irony is continued in 'They were students ...'

early Mass Roman Catholic celebration of the Eucharist.

fat lazy doctor ... indigent baby Much of the effect in this section is achieved through contrast, here between the wealthy doctor and the poor, needy baby.

smell the frying of good bacon Note the contrast between this and Kino's breakfast.

for nearly four hundred years had beaten and starved ... This refers initially to the Spanish conquest of Mexico, and perhaps to the way the natives have been subject to exploitation by foreigners.

the old language i.e. the language of the natives. As servant to a doctor, the man has risen in the world and, as so often in human nature, rejects his past. He is now too good for it.

chocolate This is made from the paste of the cacao seed.

puffy little hammocks of flesh A finely economical phrase, which conveys the decadence of the doctor. 'Hammocks' is deliberately chosen, contrasting with the natural hammock that Juana made for Coyotito.

Oriental gong A gong is a metal disc which gives a resonant note when struck, hence its use here, to summon servants.

if Masses willed and paid for out of her own estate Prayers said in mercy of her, in return for her money going into church funds.

Patron Here a respectful term meaning 'Master'.

as ugly and grey as little ulcers A clever way of implying that
just as ulcers corrupt the body, so pearls corrupt man and his
spirit. The image is used again later.

suppliant A petitioner, one who asks for something.

Chapter 2

Kino and Juana return to their home with Coyotito, and then
put out to sea in their canoe. Kino dives for oysters, brings
them up, and finds a large pearl in one of them. At this
moment they notice that the swelling is going out of Coyotito's
shoulder.

Nayarit Mountain range on the Mexican mainland, with trees
from which these special canoes were made.

lateen sail Triangular sail on long yard at an angle of 45 degrees
to the mast.

rubble of shell and algae Water-worn stones, seashells and
seaweed.

sputtered Emitted with a spitting sound. The onomatopoeic
effect is obvious.

green eel grass Submerged marine plants with long, narrow
leaves.

little sea horses The hippocampus, a genus of small fish.

spotted botete The globefish, which can distend themselves and
float belly upwards on the water.

hungry pigs i.e. wild pigs.

the sharp clarities and the vagueness of a dream Again
there is the suggestion that the experiences of life can be illusory,
ironic in view of the fact that visions attend Kino's contemplation
of the pearl.

A copper haze ... vibrate blindingly A superb visual effect
which shows Steinbeck's ability to capture in words the
experience of the senses.

diving-rock i.e. the stone used to ensure that he is 'weighted' and
drops to the sea-bed.

poultice A soft mass, here of seaweed, to apply to the inflamed part.

But the remedy lacked his authority Steinbeck is showing his knowledge of human nature here. People respect what they pay for, regardless of its effectiveness.

for the minds of people are as unsubstantial as the mirage of the Gulf That is, they do not know the truth of things, just as the 'mirage' conceals the reality (say of land shape) behind it.

This was the bed that has raised the King of Spain ... i.e. because of the rich store of pearls (and perhaps other treasure) which had been found there.

the coated grains of sand Steinbeck describes with great exactitude how pearls are formed.

by God or the gods or both Depending whether you believed in the native gods or the Christian God – or perhaps both!

the Song of the Pearl That Might Be ... the Song of the Undersea The focus here is on Kino, but the awareness and excitement is shared by many of us on the brink of discovery, in which environment, consciousness, hope and dream all play a part.

hummock A hillock or knoll.

she pretended to look away A wonderfully terse way of conveying her fear and her hope.

you must be very tactful with God or the gods Steinbeck subtly probes the simple mind here – you must keep on the right side of both if you are to get what you want.

speculatively Enquiringly.

flutes Grooves, in frills.

there were more illusions than realities A reiteration of the atmosphere of uncertainty.

incandescence Glowing with light.

as large as a seagull's egg The simile is in character, for Kino would probably think of a seagull's egg as a prize, as food.

the poison was receding from its body Ironic, since in the minds of these simple people, inherently superstitious, the pearl has brought them immediate good luck.

Chapter 3

Everyone, including the doctor, soon hears of Kino's good fortune in finding the pearl. Kino dreams of what he will do when he receives a large sum of money for it. The priest, and then the doctor, come to see him, and the doctor says that he may be able to save Coyotito, but gives the child something to make it sick, so that he will be sent for again to cure it. Later men come to the hut to try to steal the pearl, and Kino is hurt in the fight. Juana is convinced that the pearl is evil, but Kino is determined to sell it.

a thing like a colonial animal ... This whole paragraph, which compares the human body to the communal one, immediately gives a universality to the story. The experience of Kino can be seen as the experience of mankind.

there is no alms-giver in the world ... i.e. he is liable to be so overcome with his good fortune that he will be generous.

The essence of pearl ... essence of men Effective image, almost as if greed is made from a chemical reaction between human nature and the coveted object, in this case, the pearl.

the black distillate was like the scorpion ... like hunger in the smell of food ... like loneliness when love is withheld A fine sequence of images, indicating poison to the body, torture of the senses within reach of something you cannot have, and poison of the spirit by rejection.

The poison sacs of the town ... puffed with the pressure of it The comparison is with a snake, the sacs being the storehouses of poison. The central comparison is still with the nervous system and the body, both of which are subject to poison, i.e. corruption. Notice the reiteration of the closeness of man and nature, here in their evil aspects.

the Peninsula i.e. Baja (Lower) California.

pleasure-boat A boat taking people on holiday cruises, with entertainments, like gambling, on board.

lucent Shining, luminous.

Winchester carbine A type of repeating rifle, originating from the name of the American manufacturer.

whereas it is one of the greatest talents ... Steinbeck is being ironic, since it leads to covetousness, the main theme of *The Pearl*.

And electric strength had come to him He is, so to speak, charged with the power of his vision.

these things will make us free i.e. from peasanthood, from his meagre inheritance.

the music of evil ... Kino has, rightly, become suspicious, here of the priest, and always his suspicions are seen in terms of his own inner music.

threshed itself in greeting like a wind-blown flag ... and didn't see it When our own throughts absorb us, we are indifferent to others. The dog is showing its affection, but Kino is in the grip of his vision, and visions always tend to take precedence over the commonplace.

scraping crickets ... shrilling tree-frogs The sounds of nature enter into Kino's music; nature is predatory, and so is man.

like the purring of a kitten A finely selected domestic image, redolent of warmth and safety, as distinct from the natural images outside.

A plan is a real thing ... Wise appraisal, since what is thought or imagined is as real as life.

hundreds of years of subjugation were cut deep in him Another reference to the colonization of Mexico.

lymph-lined hammocks This time the image is subtly linked to the previous use of 'lymphatic' which had described Coyotito's swelling.

a liquid tone Smooth, oily, flowing persuasively.

certain ignorance ... possible knowledge A superb contrast which shows how helpless Kino is.

gelatine Transparent, tasteless, yellow substance which is formed by stewing tendons, etc.

not good at dissembling He could not conceal his real intentions.

a tightwoven school of small fishes ... a school of great fishes that drove in to eat them Again nature reflecting man in its predatory elements; big eats little, and this image is followed by another which parallels it – of hawks hunting mice.

sickness is second only to hunger The pathetic note is sounded again as commentary on those who are very poor.

He scattered the old women like chickens The implication is, of course, that they mean nothing to him.

ammonia Aqueous solution, spirit of hartshorn.

Kino's eyes were hooded now Kino is on guard, and we are reminded again of the snake imagery.

probed the night with his senses There is a sense of animal instinct here, the intuitive apprehension of something wrong.

he could feel a shell of hardness here, as with 'hooded', one is reminded of an animal protecting itself, which is precisely what Kino is reduced to doing.

the last light went out ... But Kino's brain burned Notice how the image is continued but with a different emphasis; light irradiates, but burning destroys.

a book as large as a house, with letters as big as dogs A simple image appropriately couched in the simple terms in which Kino would think.

the almost inaudible purr ... sprang like an angry cat Animal images underlining the primitive emotions which are involved. 'Scurry' further emphasizes this as the intruder flees.

a tiny light danced ... the consecrated candle With light, made by Juana from the embers, and the religious symbol of the candle, safety (one of the themes of the Song of the Family) returns. 'Consecrated' is 'set apart as sacred'.

Throw it away, Kino Woman's intuition; later Juana is to take positive action to get rid of the pearl.

break out of the pot that holds us in An odd phrase, until we remember that pots contain things, and the simple image may reflect the fact that they have few, necessary possessions, among which pots would assuredly be numbered.

mangroves Tropical trees or shrubs.

the little waves beat on the rubbly beach with an increased tempo Steinbeck always connects the moods of man with the moods of nature. Here the waves are almost keeping pace with Kino's crisis.

cozened his brain Beguiled his mind. To 'cozen' is also to 'cheat', which is directly appropriate here.

warm lucence promised a poultice ... wall ... door The images directly harmonize with the Song of the Family – they stress safety and warmth, while the poultice refers back to Coyotito's sting.

Chapter 4

Kino and the villagers go into La Paz to sell the pearl. There has been a conspiracy among the pearl dealers to keep the price down, for they are all the slaves of one man. Much is made of the strange colour of the pearl, and of its size. Kino rejects the small offers and returns to his hut. Later he steps outside, and is attacked. Juana urges him to throw the pearl back in the sea, but he decides that on the following day they will travel to the capital to sell it.

It is wonderful ... Again the connection between the individual and the community is stressed, thus giving a kind of universality to the theme.

La Paz Large port in Baja Lower California.

tithe of the first fruits of the luck Ironic use, since 'tithe' is a tax levied in support of the clergy and the church.

hung it in shimmering scarves in the air Again the idea of the physical mirage is connected to the mental mirage of Kino. 'Scarves' conceal.

the Holy Father in Rome i.e. the Pope.

all other days would take their arrangement A subtle way of getting into the consciousness, the way people think. We always feel that there are moments in time which are decisive and which will shape our future.

Kino stepped with dignity He is conscious of his new status as a pearl owner, but there is an underlying pathos in the description.

freshet-washed alley Fresh water flowing through to the sea.

belched ... spewed out Both terms are used ironically, for both convey the sense of over-indulgence rather than poverty.

And the Father ... the assaults of Hell The main theme of this paragraph is a simple acceptance of one's allotted place in life, but here it is given an ironic significance, for when Kino tries to better himself by selling the pearl he finds that the 'assaults of Hell' are both cunning and vicious.

this wall The word signifies at once the physical security of the home and the ability of the natives to draw within themselves.

barred at the windows ... only a soft gloom entered the offices Protected against burglary, but the shutting out of light, which shows off the pearls in the darkness, is ominously symbolic of death.

scarlet hibiscus A beautiful cultivated plant or shrub.

legerdemain Sleight of hand, juggling, trickery. It symbolizes quite simply here hypocrisy and cheating.

his right hand worked faster and faster Nervous reflex action at the prospect of what is to come.

as steady and cruel and unwinking as a hawk's eyes The animal association again. A hawk, like a pearl-dealer, is a predator.

the secret hand behind the desk missed in its precision Probably because he is startled at the size, and hence the value, of the pearl.

fool's gold A common mineral with a pale brass-yellow colour and brilliant metallic lustre.

a thousand pesos Silver coins, currency in the South American republics.

a little tremor of fear Probably because his game of bluff might be seen through by the bystanders, potentially hostile.

appraiser One who values, fixes the price of.

collusion Fraudulent secret understanding.

the circling of wolves, the hover of vultures From now on the animal imagery in *The Pearl* is insistent, and is usually to be equated with the worst aspects of human nature.

coagulating Clotting, curdling.

woven tules i.e. made from bulrushes.

He had lost one world and had not gained another Safety and security had gone, and he had not sold the pearl.

you have defied not the pearl-buyers ... The wide-ranging implication of Juan Tomás's words here is that no one can stand out against the established order of things.

kelp A large kind of seaweed.

like a cat's lips Animal imagery as before when Kino was threatened.

Chapter 5

Juana gets up in the night and takes the pearl. Kino wakes, goes after her, beats her, and prevents her from throwing it into the sea. Then he himself is attacked, and kills one of his attackers. He and Juana decide to leave, but as they make their way back to their hut they see that it is on fire. They shelter in Juan Tomás's house, leaving everyone to think that either they are dead or have left, and after a suitable time has elapsed, they set out.

his teeth were bared ... hissed at her like a snake ... like a sheep before the butcher Running animal images to indicate the primitive emotions roused in Kino and Juana.

walked in darkness for a moment and in light the next This symbolizes their situation, the light being warmth and safety, the darkness threat and perhaps death.

skirled The sound characteristic of bagpipes.

a wounded boat does not heal The boat is his livelihood, hence the passion of Kino's reaction.

curdled Thickening, congealing.

the smell of storm on its breath Effortless personification, but indicating the crisis to come in the elements and in the life of man.

for light was danger to him i.e. because he fears that it will expose his guilt with the discovery of the dead man.

leaked light and air Symbolic of its insecurity, vulnerability.

keening cry Sharp, mourning wail.

all darkness and shape of darkness The simple words express his bewilderment at the change of events as much as anything else.

I know I am like a leprosy Leprosy is a dreaded, chronic disease. The meaning of the phrase is 'I know that you fear that you will be associated with my guilt'.

And in that day ... safe on the water Here the elements reflect the crisis of Kino, but also provide for his disappearance – he may have been drowned in the storm.

gourd A large, fleshy fruit. The rind is emptied, dried, and used as a bottle or for storing things.

dried peppers Capsicum, picked when green or red, and used with many dishes in cooking.

plunged like frightened cattle A fine image, endowing the trees with a fearful, moving life.

little magics Ritualistic phrases, probably from the native folklore.

This pearl has become my soul Kino means that he is indelibly bound to it, it has become part of his fate.

Chapter 6

Kino, Juana and Coyotito set off, but when they have gone some distance they find that they are being followed by three trackers. They go on towards the high mountains, and shelter on a ledge, while the trackers make camp below. Kino decides that he will have to kill them. He creeps down, attacks, kills, but a shot has been fired at the little noise – a baby or a dog – high up on the ledge. Coyotito has been killed. Kino and Juana return to the village carrying his little body, and Kino throws the pearl back into the sea, where it settles among its kind.

The sky was brushed clean A very effective domestic image, almost as if Kino and Juana are in the house of nature now.

Loreto A town, with a shrine, in Baja (Lower) California.

The wind cried and whisked in the brush Appropriate personification for the mood and situation of Kino and Juana.

The coyotes Prairie dogs; but 'Coyotito' presumably means 'little dog', and the irony is that his cry brings about his death.

covert Shelter, hiding place.

brittle i.e. which could easily be snapped.

the ants moving These are symbolic of life and the ability to overcome obstacles. Ants occur at regular intervals throughout the story as a comment on human behaviour.

cricked A slight, abrupt sound, and onomatopoeic too.

resinous From resin, an adhesive substance soluble in water, and which is obtained from plants or trees.

Beware of that kind of tree... He is speaking, superstitiously of what he knows, probably to reassure himself and to remind Juana (who has disobeyed him over the pearl) that he is the lord and master.

He looked into the pearl to find his vision ... This whole paragraph should be read carefully. It brings home to Kino the truth of things, for he is seeing not vision, but reality.

the lacy shade The effect of lace is achieved by the sun coming through the gaps in the brush.

quiet as a stone An appropriate image, in view of the terrain they pass through.

as still as a sentinel Alert for any sound. Juana is guarding her young.

peeked peeped.

bighorn sheep Greyish-brown wild variety found mainly in North America.

as sensitive as hounds Ironic, since hounds are in at the kill.

as rigid as the tree limb The image again establishes man's oneness with nature.

like excited dogs on a warming trail They had got the scent and knew they were near the quarry.

the bit-roller clinked i.e. as it moved in the horse's mouth.

the tell-tale leaves Because they had fallen, they would betray their track.

ticked in protest Made little noises (as if protesting at the great heat).

erosion rubble Small stones after the wearing away of the land.

monolithic Solid block of stone shaped into a pillar or monument.

Horned toads ... little pivoting dragon heads Harmless insectivorous lizards found in California, here given an ominous aspect.

jack-rabbit, disturbed in his shape A large hare living in the open country, here moving his position because of intruders.

whining a little All the time the trackers are compared to the dogs they represent.

dry ringing of snake rattles Pit vipers have interlocking joints in the tails which rattle when vibrated.

shimmering country i.e. because of the heat haze.

Santa Rosalia Town on the coastline of the Gulf in Baja (Lower) California.

unmarkable Not capable of showing traces.

the bare stone teeth of the mountains An ominous, threatening metaphor.

did not let that consideration enter They could not think of danger, but only of the need for water.

a frowning peak Again an ominous image, a good illustration of the tightness of the writing.

maidenhair fern This has fine hairlike stalks and delicate fronds.

pampas grass Ornamental grass of South America.

water-skaters Long-legged bugs, more commonly known as water-striders.

and strewed feathers i.e. from the slaughtered birds.

Gulf The Gulf of California.

scurrying ants and behind them a larger ant An image which is repeated, and Kino knows that these human ants too will overcome any difficulties.

wind-hollowed scoops Small areas beaten into hollows by the wind.

curled up like dogs Another image used of the trackers, and, like dogs, they are close to the kill.

amulet neck-string An amulet is worn as a charm against evil.

her ancient intercession Pleading in prayer, the prayer of her race mixed with the Hail Marys of Christian prayer.

like a slow lizard The image is appropriate to the country.

germane Relevant, related to.

cicadas Transparent-winged, shrill-chirping insects.

feline Cat-like. Notice how Kino's song is part of nature, and how the chorus of nature enters into it.

as tight as wound springs The image strongly conveys his physical tension.

with a litter i.e. of puppies.

like a melon Simple simile indicating the softness of the skull when struck.

scrabbled Sideways movement.

gibbered Muttered nonsense.

cold and deadly as steel Apt image, since Kino seizes the gun, which, ironically, he has always wanted.

threw the lever The projecting piece by which the mechanism is operated.

they were not walking in single file Very significant. They have a shared grief, an equality of suffering. Kino has acknowledged that Juana was right about the pearl, but now they have reaped the tragedy of Coyotito's death because of his, Kino's, obstinacy.

She was as remote and as removed as Heaven A superb, albeit cynical, appraisal of her state: native lore and ritual and Christianity have failed her.

like well-made wooden dolls ... pillars of black fear about them Fine imagery to convey their lifelessness and the evil they have brought upon themselves by coveting the pearl.

ulcerous ... like a malignant growth Two images which go back to the body; its appearance represents a cancer of the spirit.

the music of the pearl, distorted and insane This symbolizes what life is for Kino and Juana with the death of Coyotito.

called to it and beckoned to it This fine, lyrical language expresses the message that nature is best undisturbed by man, and the pearl, soiled by violence and by corruption, returns to its natural home; while Kino and Juana, contaminated and suffering because of man, return to theirs.

Revision questions

1 Write an account of any *two* dramatic incidents in *The Pearl*, examining the way in which Steinbeck makes the atmosphere convincing.

2 What aspects of human nature are most thoroughly probed in this story? Refer closely to the text in illustration of your answer.

3 Examine any sequence or sequences of animal imagery used in *The Pearl* and show how they reflect upon character.

4 How important is the natural description to our appreciation of the story? Quote in support of your answers.

5 Write an account of Kino and his songs, and show how they contribute to our appreciation of the story.

6 What are the themes of *The Pearl*? In what ways is there optimism and pessimism in Steinbeck's treatment of them?

7 How convincing is Steinbeck's presentation of peasant life in this story? Quote in support of your answer.

8 Write a character study of Kino, indicating whether you consider him psychologically true to life.

9 How important is Juana's role in the story? Select incidents where you think her influence is felt.

10 Write an essay on any *two* or *three* aspects of Steinbeck's style which you think are important.

11 In what ways is *The Pearl* a parable?

12 Write an essay in appreciation of the poetic elements of *The Pearl*.

13 What does the pearl itself symbolize?

14 In what ways does Steinbeck convey the relationship between man and nature?

15 Write an essay on the moral elements in *The Pearl*, showing how Steinbeck makes his own presence felt in the story.

Pan study aids Titles published in the Brodie's Notes series

W. H. Auden Selected Poetry

Jane Austen Emma Mansfield Park Northanger Abbey Persuasion
Pride and Prejudice

Anthologies of Poetry Ten Twentieth Century Poets The Poet's
Tale

Samuel Beckett Waiting for Godot

Arnold Bennett The Old Wives' Tale

William Blake Songs of Innocence and Experience

Robert Bolt A Man for All Seasons

Harold Brighouse Hobson's Choice

Charlotte Brontë Jane Eyre

Emily Brontë Wuthering Heights

Robert Browning Selected Poetry

John Bunyan The Pilgrim's Progress

Geoffrey Chaucer (parallel texts) The Franklin's Tale The Knight's
Tale The Miller's Tale The Nun's Priest's Tale The Pardoner's Tale
Prologue to the Canterbury Tales The Wife of Bath's Tale

Richard Church Over the Bridge

John Clare Selected Poetry and Prose

Samuel Taylor Coleridge Selected Poetry and Prose

Wilkie Collins The Woman in White

William Congreve The Way of the World

Joseph Conrad The Nigger of the Narcissus & Youth The Secret
Agent

Charles Dickens Bleak House David Copperfield Dombey and Son
Great Expectations Hard Times Little Dorrit Oliver Twist
Our Mutual Friend A Tale of Two Cities

Gerald Durrell My Family and Other Animals

George Eliot Middlemarch The Mill on the Floss Silas Marner

T. S. Eliot Murder in the Cathedral Selected Poems

John Milton A Choice of Milton's Verse Comus and Samson
Agonistes Paradise Lost I, II

Sean O'Casey Juno and the Paycock The Shadow of a Gunman and
The Plough and the Stars

George Orwell Animal Farm 1984

John Osborne Luther

Alexander Pope Selected Poetry

Siegfried Sassoon Memoirs of a Fox-Hunting Man

Peter Shaffer The Royal Hunt of the Sun

William Shakespeare Antony and Cleopatra As You Like It
Coriolanus Hamlet Henry IV (Part I) Henry IV (Part II)
Henry V Julius Caesar King Lear King Richard III
Love's Labour's Lost Macbeth Measure for Measure
The Merchant of Venice A Midsummer Night's Dream
Much Ado about Nothing Othello Richard II Romeo and Juliet
The Sonnets The Taming of the Shrew The Tempest
Twelfth Night The Winter's Tale

G. B. Shaw Androcles and the Lion Arms and the Man
Caesar and Cleopatra The Doctor's Dilemma Pygmalion Saint Joan

Richard Sheridan Plays of Sheridan: The Rivals; The Critic;
The School for Scandal

John Steinbeck The Grapes of Wrath Of Mice and Men & The
Pearl

Tom Stoppard Rosencrantz and Guildenstern are Dead

J. M. Synge The Playboy of the Western World

Jonathan Swift Gulliver's Travels

Alfred Tennyson Selected Poetry

William Thackeray Vanity Fair

Flora Thompson Lark Rise to Candleford

Dylan Thomas Under Milk Wood

Anthony Trollope Barchester Towers

Mark Twain Huckleberry Finn

Keith Waterhouse Billy Liar

Evelyn Waugh Decline and Fall Scoop

H. G. Wells The History of Mr Polly

John Webster The White Devil

Oscar Wilde The Importance of Being Earnest

Virginia Woolf To the Lighthouse

William Wordsworth The Prelude (Books 1, 2)
Wordsworth Selections

W. B. Yeats Selected Poetry

Australian titles

George Johnston My Brother Jack

Thomas Keneally The Chant of Jimmie Blacksmith

Ray Lawler Summer of the Seventeenth Doll

Henry Lawson The Bush Undertaker & Selected Short Stories

Ronald McKie The Mango Tree

Kenneth Slessor Selected Poems

Ralph Stow The Merry-Go-Round in the Sea To the Islands

Patrick White The Tree of Man

David Williamson The Removalists

Students' notes